From *Fear* to Freedom

From Fear to Freedom

THE TRANSFORMATION OF YUNA-LAND

by
Marjorie Pethybridge

Nenge Books, Australia

From Fear to Freedom
by Marjorie Pethybridge

Copyright © Marjorie Pethybridge 1970

All rights reserved

This book or parts thereof may not be reproduced in any form, stored in a mechanical retrieval system or transmitted in any form by any means - electronic, mechanical, recording, photocopy or otherwise - without prior written permission of the publisher.

First edition ISBN 0551005610

Second edition - Design, desktop by Nenge Books
Published by Nenge Books, Australia, August 2021
ABN 26809396184
nengebooks1@gmail.com
www.nengebooks.com

Photos by Ivor & Marjorie Pethybridge, Richard Pethybridge, Ted Crawford. Used by permission.

All Scripture quotations, unless otherwise indicated, are taken from the Holy Bible, New International Version®, NIV®. Copyright ©1973, 1978, 1984, 2011 by Biblica, Inc.™ Used by permission of Zondervan. All rights reserved worldwide. www.zondervan.com The "NIV" and "New International Version" are trademarks registered in the United States Patent and Trademark Office by Biblica, Inc.™

Scriptures and additional materials marked "GNB" are quoted from the Good News Bible © 1994 published by the Bible Societies/HarperCollins Publishers Ltd UK, Good News Bible© American Bible Society 1966, 1971, 1976, 1992. Used with permission.

Scripture quotations marked "Phillips" are taken from The New Testament in Modern English, copyright © 1958, 1959, 1960 J.B. Phillips and 1947, 1952, 1955, 1957. The Macmillian Company, New York. Used by permission. All rights reserved.

Nenge Books publishes quality books using cost effective print-on-demand technology to enable independent authors to publish. Enquiries from authors are welcomed.

ISBN 978-0-6488206-8-0

Contents

Foreword	vi
Introduction to the Second Edition	ix
1. BATTLEGROUND	1
2. FORWARD WITH CHRIST	9
To the Highlands	10
To Koroba	15
To Pori	23
3. A WORK BEGINS	53
Murder!	54
A Handmade Airstrip	59
Play Day	72
One Day at a Time	76
Local Preachers	83
Sowing the Word	88
Early Reactions	90
4. FEAR OF THE DEVIL	97
In Sickness	98
The Women's Story	104
A Girl's Life	114
A Man's Life	118

5. FREEDOM IN CHRIST	123
First Fruits	124
Reaping a Full Harvest	135
The First Fetish Burning	140
Establishing Churches	143
The First Elders	149
Decentralisation	151
Literacy	154
Why?—and How?	157
Reaching Out	161
Missionaries of CMML	170
Abbreviations	171

Foreword

Seven years in retrospect does not seem long, but tremendous, far-reaching changes often take place within a short span of time. Take for example, the first few years following Pentecost or the three years following the recent attempted coup in Indonesia. Certainly, radical changes have occurred in Yuna-land. Marjorie Pethybridge has documented some of those which have occurred in the narrow Pori Valley between Tari and Lake Kopiago in the heart of what is now Papua New Guinea and astride the former Papua-New Guinea border.

In October 1962, I stood with the husband of the author on a steep mountainside overlooking the Pori Valley, with a line of yodelling Huli tribesman behind us. In faith, we claimed the people of the valley for Christ. Faith on a pioneer mission field is never divorced from hard work, and the Pori Valley has been no exception. The Pethybridge, Dobbie and McCullough families, Ron Whitehead, Infant Welfare Sister Betty Gillam and volunteer builders have all shared in the hard manual and spiritual battles, and today the changes are apparent. In place of a bush shack at the end of a two-day journey over the mountains, stands an airstrip literally carved out of the mountainside, three sawn-timber houses (the result of months of pit-sawing, chain-sawing and milling), a large church building, a school, and dispensary. In place of dark, suspicious glances, sudden violence and an atmosphere of fear, is a pleasant openness and freedom. A few months ago, I was present when delegates from the Yuna churches met with their former traditional enemies from the Huli churches in a neighbouring valley to discuss church problems and the application of New Testament principles to their society and culture. The spiritual discernment of some of the men was quite remarkable. "From Fear to Freedom" is certainly a fitting and accurate title for this book.

Wonderful is the transformation in many lives, but the work has only begun. A tremendous amount of consolidation is necessary. Bible translation has only begun. Literacy programmes are in their infancy. There is a demand for education in English for the children. The people will face, in increasing measure, the pressures and tensions of a changing culture as they are caught up in the accelerating development of a country awaking and emerging from the Stone Age into the twentieth century. The pioneering days are passing and new missionaries with different gifts are required to fill the ranks—Bible teachers with linguistic ability to establish the Christians firmly in the faith and school teachers to prepare the rising generation for Christian leadership in a changing situation. Without such, the spiritual advances here recorded may be dissipated and lost. May the reading of this book challenge young men and women, nationals as well as expatriates, to train and prepare themselves for such work.

Kay W. Liddle
Wewak, Papua New Guinea
1969

Introduction to the Second Edition

Almost sixty years have gone by since Ivor and Marjorie Pethybridge first trekked into the Pori Valley. And some 50 years have passed since the first edition of *From Fear to Freedom* was published. Copies of that first edition have long been unavailable for the next generation to know the history of the dramatic events that surrounded Ivor and Marjorie's pioneer entry into the Pori Valley and settling among the local Yuna-speaking people. That story needs to be re-told to the next generation who have grown up in a Christian environment. As Grace Kenamu said when read this book after visiting Jenny and me in our home several years ago, "This is our history. We should have it in writing in our hands." That comment has been the motivation for this second edition.

Some updating and minor corrections have been made from the original story. For example, outside government and mission contact came through the Huli area to the east and south. The Huli called their neighbours the "Duna", but the people call themselves "Yuna". We have agreed to call these people "Yuna", even though Pori is located near the boundary between the two languages and many people nearby speak both languages.

We honour the vision, the faith and devotion to Jesus Christ of Ivor and Marjorie and their missionary colleagues who facilitated the "advance" into the Yuna valleys of the Papua New Guinea highlands in the early 1960s. For the sake of history, we have appended a list of the CMML missionaries referred to in this story.

Many changes have come in the last 50 years. The Pori airstrip, always so marginal as the story reveals, and built with so much pains-taking effort, has been permanently closed. A vehicular road now connects the valley to the outside world. The Christian Brethren Churches of Papua New Guinea now look after the former mission station as a Christian Centre with a primary school, a high school, a health centre, a Bible School and other community facilities located on it. The country itself has become an independent nation and many descendants of the people Marjorie Pethybridge writes about now live in other parts of the country, some having pursued education elsewhere, even overseas. Many educated Yuna people hold responsible positions in government and business.

This book was written by a pioneer Christian missionary from the Gospel-bearer's perspective. It is over to the Gospel hearers, both Yuna and other Papua New Guinean people, to write their complementary and continuing story of Gospel challenges in their emerging community and nation.

Thanks go to a number of people who have helped with this second edition. In particular, I mention Ivor and Marjorie's son, Richard, who has taken a personal interest in this production and has supplied many of the photos. My personal thanks to Marjorie's grandson, Jordan Betteridge, who typed up the manuscript for this edition. Former MAF pilot Ted Crawford supplied several photos of early Cessna plane landings at Pori. Sisi Fountain, my niece-in-law, has produced much improved maps relevant to this story. Michael Steer also assisted me with proof-reading. Deep appreciation to all these folk and others not personally named.

Ossie Fountain
Titahi Bay, New Zealand
July 2021

1

BATTLEGROUND

We are not fighting against people made of flesh and blood, but against persons without bodies—evil princes of darkness who rule this world, and against huge numbers of wicked spirits in the spirit world.

Ephesians 6:12: (Phillips)

"Over my dead body!" The *glasman*[1] glared defiance.

"But, Purua," reasoned Ivor, "It's the only suitable timber within carrying distance."

"No matter," he doggedly held his point. "You'll fell that timber over my dead body. Keep Out!"

The group nodded their assent, their faces expressionless masks. They were standing together on the airstrip under a black, threatening sky. I could hear their voices drifting up to me, mingled with the rumbling thunder. Nor was it the first time I had witnessed such a scene. Over the last eighteen months, Ivor had tried again and again to reason with the men who lived to the south east of us. All we wanted was the milling rights to a patch of bush. Always it ended with that exasperating "No!" and no reasons given.

As I paused to watch from halfway up the track that day, I saw Purua come to the fore. I could not recall that he had taken part before. Now as I watched I wondered. Could it be that he was responsible for that unrelenting, "No!"?

Walking on up the track, I recalled scenes I had witnessed of another *glasman* when he communicated with the spirits, and recalled some of the fragments of information that Ivor had gathered about Purua's doings from some of the older men who were willing to talk. Such a *glasman* was called in by the tribe in times of sickness.

Purua, I knew, had the people in such a bondage of fear that he had only to state his price to get it. He was a heartless old rogue; the more desperate someone's plight, the greater was his

---

1.. Melanesian Tok Pisin for a person who communicates with the spirits.

opportunity of gain. Nobody argued with him; they just agreed with his demands so that he might move off quickly to his private shrine to commune with the demons.

I could imagine him crouching there with his paraphernalia all around him: a pile of sacred stones, pieces of pearl shell, a string of small shells, and blood-stained holes where previous sacrifices had been made and the blood carefully caught. Pervading all, an atmosphere of intense evil.

I recalled vividly seeing an old *glasman* enter the spirit world to find out which of the spirits was the aggrieved one that was causing the illness. He was a gaunt, wizened old man with a ragged beard and matted hair, crouching on his haunches, cupping a few leaves in both hands. He blew on them, muttered, blew again and then his whole being was gripped by something sinister and frightening as he listened for a reply.

After that, Purua would collect and sacrifice the pig that the relatives of the sick one had brought. This time he prayed directly to the spirit that had been named, and the patient was healed. If there was no sign of improvement, Purua had failed, through no fault of his own, to get the right name. So the whole performance was repeated until either the patient died or the relatives were poverty-stricken.

There was a sound outside of boots being scraped on the stones and Ivor entered our thatched cottage. Wearily he slumped into a chair and I made him a cup of tea. It always took it out of him when he had to deal with one of these interminable arguments.

"Well, now I know why they won't sell the bush to us," he sighed. "See the top of that large pine right in the centre? Purua's shrine is at the base of it."

"So it is he," I thought to myself. "This is going to mean a lot of trouble."

Ivor was speaking again. "I see now that this is not just a matter of persuading the men to co-operate. It is a spiritual issue affecting the whole future of the work of God here. We just have to win out."

Truly it was not just a battle of wills with Purua and his intimidated followers, but a spiritual battle to be fought and won. I remembered Ephesians 6:12:

We are not fighting against people made of flesh and blood, but against persons without bodies—evil princes of darkness who rule this world, and against huge numbers of wicked spirits in the spirit world. (Phillips).

This was our situation exactly. The evil princes of darkness were present as we bowed our heads scarcely able to pray. What a fearful thing satanic oppression is. And we felt that we really were up against huge numbers of wicked spirits in our isolated situation that day. How glad we were to know that we could claim victory in the name of him who had already won the victory at the Cross.

While we were still at prayer we had a visit from a Yuna youth called Tiaga. He had had some training in medical work and ran a little aid post further down the valley. While away training, he had been influenced by Lutheran missionaries and was sympathetic with us as we told him about Purua and the bush.

He had not been initiated into the ways of evil spirit worship, but knew the power that it held over the tribe. Having seen something of the more advanced areas of the territory, he knew that it would be to his people's advantage to co-operate. The three of us prayed and then Tiaga said, "I'm going down to talk with Purua and the others." Quietly we watched him go. Though a mature lad, he was no match for Purua's subtle evil and we returned again to prayer. If only God would triumph, it would surely be the beginning of a mighty change for the people of the Pori valley.

And He did.

God worked another miracle.

Dramatically Purua changed his mind.

The battle ceased. Christ was victor in his heart, and Purua decided to forsake the ways of the evil spirits and to seek God.

The men concerned were called together again. Purua said, "Sell the cutting rights to the missionary." They obeyed, and the next morning the trees began to fall in preparation for milling. Eventually the sacred pine fell too and was used for the lining of our lounge.

Purua immediately attended every meeting he could get to. In only a few short weeks there was an obvious change in his appearance. We watched and, with our prayer partners in New Zealand, prayed, taking every opportunity to befriend him. One Sunday afternoon, sitting cross-legged on our kitchen floor, he confessed his sin to God. What a blood chilling list it was: murder, immorality, witchcraft and, above all, almost daily communion with the evil spirits.

"I've talked directly with Satan," he said. "Please Jesus, wash my heart clean." As he found complete cleansing in the blood of Christ, a new life welled up within. Purua was transformed.

Immediately he had a tireless radiant witness for his Saviour. The break with his former way of life left him with much time on his hands. He used it all to witness to folk who kept coming to him with requests to commune with the evil spirits. He began travelling around amongst former enemies, fellow spirit-men and clients, showing love instead of instilling terror, teaching freedom in place of fear, gossiping the gospel everywhere he could. His radiant face and utterly changed way of life made everyone look and listen.

Purua, who, through all his life was held in slavery by his fear of death, found for himself the freedom which God's children enjoy. Hebrews 2:15 and Romans 8:21.

The Southern Highlands in the 1960s

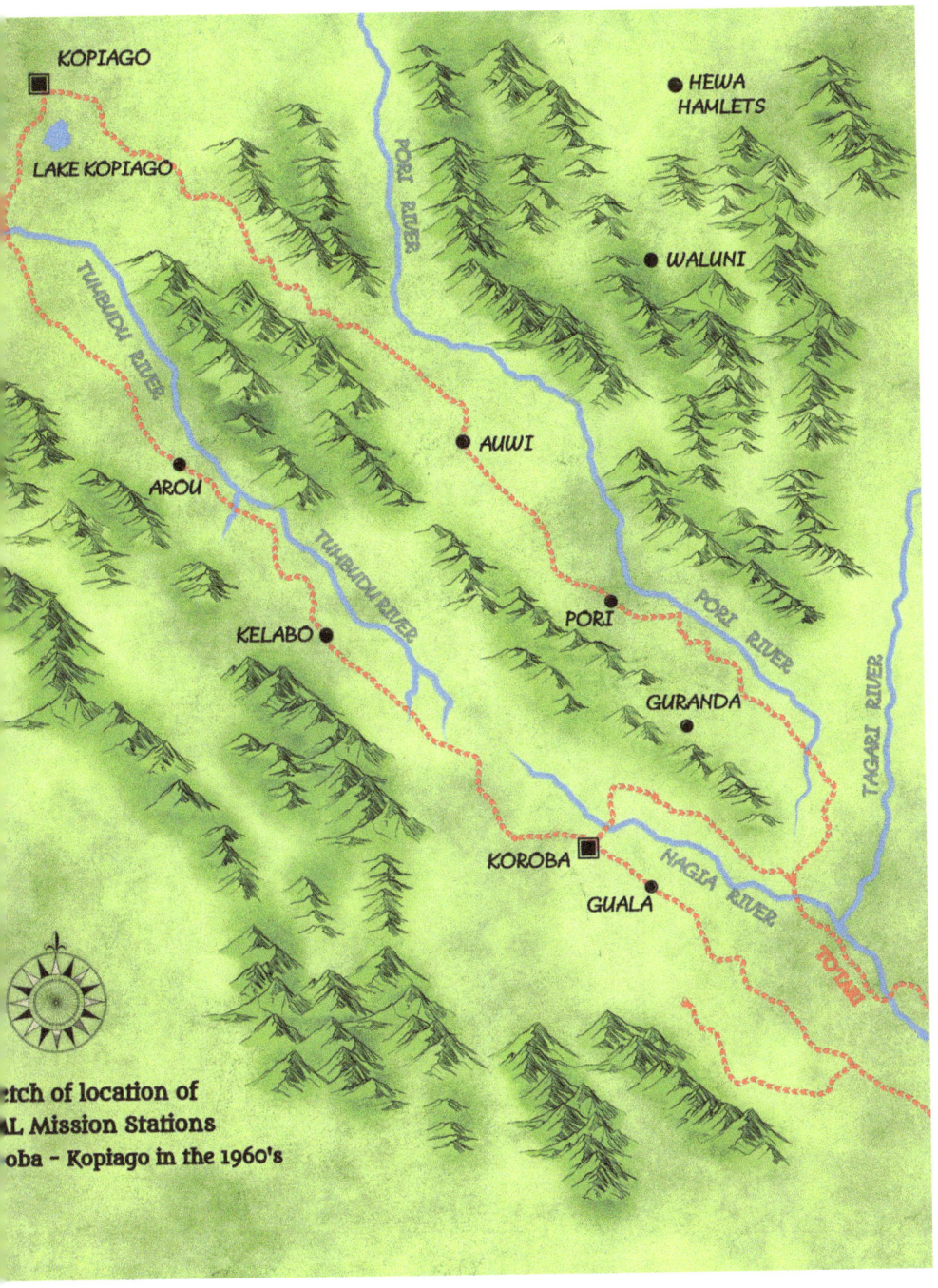

2

FORWARD WITH CHRIST

> The Spirit of the Sovereign Lord is upon me,
> because the Lord has anointed me
> to proclaim good news to the poor.
> He has sent me to bind up the brokenhearted,
> to proclaim freedom for the captives…
>
> Isaiah 61:1

To the Highlands

Late 1958–September 1961

He sat there staring across the room at me, one of his eyes seeming to look right through me. He was horribly cross-eyed. Sitting on a form in Twyman's house at Tari in the Highlands of Papua New Guinea one wet mid-day, I was face to face with the first Yuna I had ever seen. Although the one eye seemed to be fixed on me, he was in fact giving all his attention to the missionary couple behind the table at the end of the room.

I knew everyone else in the room. They were Huli tribal elders. This Yuna man was just visiting one of them. It was the first time he had met a missionary or heard anything of his message. The Huli men had been listening to the Gospel for several years. Now they met to face the decision on what they were going to do about it. Would they forsake animism and the worship of evil spirits? Dare they become Christians?

"Who is this God you talk about?" one asked.

"He is the One who made everything, earth, sun, food, you yourselves too."

"But how can we be sure that He is stronger than the spirits? We have always had to appease them. We know their power."

"Dare we forsake them now?" another voice said, expressing fear mingled with a tinge of hope.

"Many brown-skinned folk like yourselves have done so," the missionary replied understandingly. "As they forsake the spirits, they prove for themselves that God is real and stronger than Satan and all his evil spirits. Worshipping God brings freedom from the fear of the spirits. He makes you happy too, and at peace with other people."

Several hours went by. Bible verses were discussed.

"We and our ancestors have always killed pigs to the spirits. We appease them in many different ways every day of our lives. Can we really be free of it all? We certainly would like to be." Another cautious voice joined in for the first time, "Even if we risk this change ourselves, what of our children? We must protect them from the reprisals of the spirits."

The missionary answered, "God does give freedom from fear. He loves you all. He will care for your children too. You trust Him."

The crossed eyes were terror-stricken. These were all new concepts to him. He had walked several days to visit Piru and never before heard the name of God. Forsake the spirits? 'Impossible!' his expressive face screamed silently.

"He is a Yuna," I was told.

"Yuna?" I asked. "Who and where are they?"

"They are neighbours of the Huli, starting about 50 kilometres west of Tari. There are several thousand of them with another language from the Huli, though probably a similar culture. A number are bi-lingual like Piru's friend. There have been a few Government patrols through the area, but they are still uncontrolled, frightened, fighting, and in bondage to the spirits."

⋊

Three years later, Ivor and I were at Amanab in the West Sepik District relieving the Austins for furlough. They were due back soon and we were asking the Lord where we were to go next. I had prayed for the Yuna people since meeting one of them. Now their need became a personal issue.

One day Max Flavel, Field Superintendent of Missionary Aviation Fellowship, flew in and, as we stood chatting on the airstrip he commented: "You two were in the Southern Highlands before, weren't you?"

"That's right," Ivor assented.

"Then you know the type of people and density of population up there. I was flying over those valleys west of Tari the other day. There must be thousands there with no missionary." There was silence as he paused, then he added feelingly, "Why isn't somebody going into them?" A few minutes later, the little yellow Cessna roared off down the strip and turned east for Wewak.

Ivor was silent as we walked back up to the house. I guessed what his thoughts would be. I knew what mine were. The Lord had challenged us both through Max's direct words. Ivor said nothing for a couple of days though I imagined how he was praying. Then it all came out. At breakfast as he ate from a halved pineapple, he suddenly said, "You know, I can't get that Yuna situation out of my mind. I've prayed and thought and prayed and thought."

He looked at me with a question mark on his face. "Yes, me too," I said. We began seeking the Lord's guidance together. The very next mail brought a circular from Kay Liddle with a report on a visit he had made to the Southern Highlands. The area was soon to be de-restricted, thus allowing missionaries to move in. The Government Officer he had interviewed was keen for our missionaries to come. Later Kay visited us. Quite unaware of our exercise, or even interest, he felt that he should come and put to us the possibility of our going to the Yuna people.

There was always a fair bit of banter when Kay and Ivor got together. This time was no exception. Two people could hardly be more different, Ivor a farmer and practical, Kay an accountant and a thinker, but the ragging went back and forth with reminiscences of hilarity during their Bible Training Institute days together.

Before Kay left the next morning, we took him into our confidence. He was thrilled to see the Lord already at work and it was good to have him praying with us. The Lord had given us no peace about remaining in the Amanab area. Now, regarding the Yuna, the increasing evidence seemed to say: "This is the way; walk in it."

A few weeks later we gathered at Anguganak for the annual conference of missionaries of the Open Brethren Assemblies (whose missions in many countries of the world were registered as Christian Missions in Many Lands (CMML) with over two thousand missionaries). Kay, as Chairman of the meeting, outlined to the group the situation in the Southern Highlands. The Government was planning to open up the area, occupied by the Yuna tribe, to Europeans.

"What are we going to do about these unreached people? They certainly present a challenge," he said, "but last year we agreed that we should not open up any new stations. There just aren't enough of us to consolidate what we have already begun."

A voice spoke up from the side of the room. "But could it be the Lord's time for us to start expanding now? Is He challenging us to step out in faith? Surely He will supply the needed workers?" A buzz of conversation swept around the room. The discussion continued to and fro.

Finally, the Chairman summarised: "If we move into the Highlands there will be rapid growth, resulting in several mission stations, and a number of missionaries will be needed. We will have to consider medical and school work, the building of houses, chapels, roads and airstrips, besides a strenuous trekking programme to reach the people. Some of our plans for the Sepik will have to be sacrificed."

Ivor and I listened with interest to all of the discussion and then told how the Lord had been leading us. It was unanimously decided to reserve a decision until all had had time to pray about it. Little did we realise that Kay and Gwen Liddle had long been concerned about the Southern Highlands personally, but had not been ready to make their interest known while they still had the full responsibility at Green River.

The group met again after several days and all with one accord spoke of their certainty that this move was definitely what God had planned. Kay and Gwen told us all how the Lord had been guiding them into this move. Then the Edens and Fosters agreed to move to Green River together – and the Highlands advance was on. Each and all of us were conscious of a deep pressure of the Holy Spirit compelling us to launch out. It was a wonderful experience of the Lord meeting with us all in a special way for a special purpose.

"The Lord is leading us," Ivor said to me, "there is no doubt about that, but we will be attacking Satan's stronghold and he will not take it sitting down either." Looking at our inadequacies, the future loomed alarmingly before us. It seemed an impossible task. But then, looking at His abundance, we realised by faith that we were fully equipped.

I will build My church and the gates of Hades will not overcome it, was one verse that He gave us. So we packed up at Amanab, handed everything back to the Austins, then moved out to the beach at Wewak to prepare ourselves for the advance.

The Lord met all our needs. Physically, we relaxed and felt refreshed. Materially, money came in from missionaries, businessmen, farmers, pensioners and even children. Spiritually, the Lord was encouraging and preparing us from His Word. Much prayer ascended for us. Hundreds of relatives and informed Christians claimed the Yuna people for Christ. One verse became especially mine at that time:

And God is able to bless you abundantly, so that in all things at all times, having all that you need, you will abound in every good work.

2 Corinthians 9:8

To Koroba

September 1961–January 1962

The camera was focused on a group of carriers struggling across a cane swing-bridge. The river was wide, and strong stays were well buried on either bank. Cane vines spanned the space, held together by dozens of smaller vines. The whole thing looked like a huge hammock. Uneven-sized saplings laid long-ways formed the decking and, below, muddy water leaped high against jagged boulders.

Crack!

It sounded like one of the taut vines snapping. A mighty shout of fear rent the air, and the view-finder blurred wildly as the men rushed either way to firm ground.

The carriers milled around, talking nervously. It was some time before Kay and Ivor were able to get them all across, this time ensuring that they went over singly—a precaution they realised should have been taken in the first place. Finally, with everyone gathered on the far bank, they paused to thank God. It could so well have been a tragedy.

This was but one of the many colourful incidents that Ivor and Kay experienced in those first few weeks in the Highlands. They had set out from Wewak in September 1961. Taking off with Missionary Aviation Fellowship one morning, they were glad that it was fine enough to see the coast and the great Sepik River Plains. As the plane climbed up to 12,000 feet (about 3,660 metres), they crossed the central ranges of mountains, all heaped up together with their giant limestone faces, sharp pinnacles of rock, and high waterfalls. Suddenly they dropped down fast into the Tari basin, one and a half hours flying time south of Wewak and right in the centre of the main island of New Guinea.

It was cold. The change from steamy Wewak to the Tari valley floor at 1,675 metres altitude was a sudden one. However, the welcome at the Unevangelised Fields Mission (UFM) station was warm. After a few days of chatting things over, and visiting Government Officials at Tari, they went on 40 kilometres by road to the Koroba Patrol Post, still in the Huli language group, but within a few hours' trekking time of the Yuna people. Nearby was an out-station of the Methodist Overseas Mission staffed by two Melanesians, a pastor and a teacher. They were given the use of an old house at the Government station. It was a great barn of a place with a two-metre fireplace that ate whole logs at a time—very cosy when it was wet and cold almost every afternoon.

The Government Officer gave his time to study maps and population figures with them. He gave them every help including his recommendation that they be granted permits to survey the Yuna valleys under his care. As the area was still restricted territory, it was closed to Europeans. This was a precaution that the Territory of Papua and New Guinea administration took until they had reasonable control in uncontrolled areas. The permits were issued by District Headquarters.

The very next morning Kay and Ivor set out to survey Yuna-land. They took several men to carry food and bedding and headed for the Pori Valley. Over the first mountain range they descended to Guranda by midday and were met by quite a few men and boys. They were friendly and willingly went off to collect firewood, water, and sweet potatoes for them. Soon they were set up in the 'rest house'. (A group of three or four grass huts were built at stages throughout uncontrolled areas for the use of Government Officers on patrol with their policemen and carriers. Missionaries were also free to make use of them.)

Surveying the surrounding country, Ivor said to Kay, "I'd hate to be looking for an airstrip site here."

"No hope at all," said Kay. "There just isn't a piece of flat land to be seen."

Late in the afternoon, a number of men came to visit them. Through an interpreter, they were able to tell these visitors a little of who God was—the One who created everything, including the sun which the Huli people worshipped as creator. The men gave them a puzzled but interested hearing.

The following morning was crisp and clear as they struggled up and down steep hills for a couple of hours to reach the area where the Huli and Yuna tribes overlapped. After that the valley widened out and the population increased. The area was covered with sweet potato gardens, scrub, great outcrops of limestone and acres of kunai grass with no formed tracks. They could find no drinking water.

The Pori Valley headman came to escort them in. When he realised that they were keeping a lookout for an airstrip site, he expressed fear that they might be angry with him for being unable to locate one. Stopping for lunch, they were quickly surrounded by a group of men and boys. Apparently, they were expecting them. The message had been yodelled and shouted from hilltop to hilltop the evening before. Enthusiastically, the men begged Kay and Ivor to return and settle.

After a night at Ayuguali rest house, they decided to return home by a different route, thus seeing more of the area. The way chosen went directly over the mountains without returning up the valley at all. They rued their choice. With no real track, they had to clamber over outcrops of limestone or steep razor-back ridges. At times every step had to be carefully calculated, then tested. One false move could have spelt disaster, with the ground falling away hundreds of metres below.

Down out of the mountains at last, there was no respite. They now had to scramble along through old fighting ditches.

These were over three metres deep and one metre wide and criss-crossed most of the valley, their tops carefully camouflaged and with sharp pointed sticks in the mud below. They had been formidable barriers to the enemy and concealed routes to the initiated. This day was nine and a half hours of the toughest walking Ivor had experienced in seven years of trekking in various parts of the Territory of Papua and New Guinea.

Back in the old house at Koroba, they rested over the weekend, then headed off early Monday morning to survey the Tumbudu Valley. It took three and a half hours to reach the Huli-Yuna boundary. With the road partly formed some of the way, it was comparatively easy walking. Contacts were friendly and gardens became more plentiful as they moved in. Coming to a new 'rest house', they decided to stop there overnight and had friendly contacts with the people.

The next morning dawned dismally and they waited in the cold fog for fresh carriers to gather, then set out in steady rain through broken country over unformed tracks deep with mud. They crossed several rivers, jumping from stone to slippery stone, or balancing along precarious logs. The largest ones were spanned by cane swing bridges.

At midday it was still raining—great cold, wet sheets of it, so they boiled the billy in a hut four metres by four, scarcely high enough to clear their heads when sitting down. Thirty men and boys crammed in too. Then someone started an argument over an old pig payback. He had spotted an old enemy. Here was his chance to show his strength in front of a large group of men. He shrieked at him that he had not paid enough compensation when he had killed his uncle years before.

Frightened but defiant, the accused shouted back, "The compensation was adequate, the tribal elders agreed that it was. I paid many pigs to your clan."

"You did not pay me enough. I demand a large sow from you immediately."

"I have no large sow."

"You owe it to me."

"I do not."

"You do. Find one for me or someone will die."

Everyone began shouting at once, their hands automatically reaching to their axe or bone dagger. Finally, the interpreter's voice penetrated the noise. When he had their attention he reminded them that the Government Officer in Koroba had told them to bring their dispute to him to be settled peaceably. It took a few unnerving minutes to quieten them down. Eventually they got the carriers under way again. Still in heavy rain, they clambered up and down slippery slopes, in and out of dripping bush and across the Tumbudu River. What a relief it was to see the Kelabo 'rest house' by half past three in the afternoon.

They spent the next day investigating airstrip sites. From various vantage points, they found two possibilities and hacked a path down the centre through the scrub and bamboo for the full length of a runway (460 metres). Both seemed likely places and it was cheering to have the co-operation of all the headmen from quite an area around. They wanted the prestige and material advantages of having a white man come to settle amongst them.

The next day they returned to Koroba and asked Missionary Aviation Fellowship to come in for an aerial survey.

Mountains leaned outwards and rivers rushed uphill as the pilot took them for a close look at Yuna-land in a little Cessna 180. It was always quite an experience to be up in a tiny plane, trying to see immediately below in narrow valleys, with steep mountains towering either side. It was a case of mind over matter to forget the ups and downs of one's stomach and concentrate. They realised that there was a much denser population than was apparent to the ground patrols, especially in the Pori Valley's main population. This aerial survey convinced them of the room and need for several mission stations, each with a number of missionaries to reach the Yuna tribe.

During the following week they flew to established centres in the Highlands and interviewed Government officials, getting data regarding population distribution, the location of tribes without missionaries, and the possible date of de-restriction of these areas.

With the different Mission leaders they discussed the plans, if any, of each particular mission for working among the Yuna people, then returned to Tari.

They were very much cast on the Lord, knowing that they must now decide where to settle. The Lord spoke out of His Word, encouraging them from Joshua.

Be strong...take possession of the land the Lord your God is giving you...I am with you.   Joshua 1:9,11

Let the peace of God be umpire in your hearts.

Philippians. 4:7.

The One who calls you is faithful, and He will do it.

1 Thessalonians. 5:24.

There was not long to wait.

Out at the UFM station they prayed over the whole situation. How they appreciated the help and co-operation given by the missionaries there!

Late that afternoon the Acting Chairman of the Methodist Overseas Mission in the Southern Highlands District called on them. "We are experiencing serious staffing difficulties," he explained. "Several of our senior staff are ill and their return to Papua New Guinea is uncertain. We had planned to have a European on our Koroba out-station by now, but there is no possibility of anyone being available for a long time yet."

Then, "Would you consider taking it over from us?" It was like a bombshell. Ivor and Kay looked at each other. Already they had realised the necessity of a base at Koroba for some time to come, in order to be able to establish a work among the Yuna. Was the Lord now saying, "Are you prepared to trust Me for a permanent work among the Huli at Koroba as well?" Their hearts responded, "This is it. This is of the Lord." And what a provision it was!

The Solomons pastor and Rabaul teacher had already broken into the initial barriers of animism. Their excellent conduct had done much to gain the people's ears and confidence. They had a medical and school work in progress, as well as a preaching programme. Several temporary buildings were erected, there was a stack of pit-sawn timber ready for dressing for permanent buildings and an airstrip was nearing completion. Here was the needed base with a mission station and spiritual work already under way. So the Lord gave them the land.

Two days later, they gave their answer to the Methodist Overseas Mission. It was arranged that their pastors would stay on until Ivor and Kay could build a home each and get to know some of the people a little.

"A great opportunity has opened for an effective work," Ivor quoted in faith when passing the wonderful news on to me by letter. "Koroba itself will develop into a big work," he envisaged. "There is a dense population of thousands barely touched with the Gospel."

Arrangements were made for supplies to be flown in to Tari, and then Ivor took them through to Koroba in the Methodist tractor and trailer. They worked from dawn to dark for the next two months, all the while living in a dirt-floored, windowless shack they called 'the black hole'. The Methodist workers had each commenced a home for themselves, and Ivor and Kay were able in that time to finish these off, with some additions. They each consisted of three small rooms in a straight line, low to the ground. With the big overhang of the thatched roof, it was not possible to see out of the windows when standing up. They added a kitchen and bathroom on to the back of one for the Liddles, and then built an iron-roofed laundry for water catchment at the back of ours with a bathroom at one end of it, just a few yards from our back door.

Right on Christmas, they returned to the Sepik for discussion with other missionaries and a break before returning with their families, to get under way with a full-scale missionary programme at Koroba.

It was a great day when the first white missionary women arrived to settle at Koroba. The women and girls flocked around me. The next morning, Sunday, they were there at 7 a.m. to escort me to the ten o'clock service. I had previously studied Huli for a year and had been revising it while waiting in the Sepik. Now I was able to converse with them and commence women's meetings as well as take over the medical work from the Methodist teacher who was now leaving.

Yes, they flocked around me when I arrived, but the scene on the day when Gwen Liddle arrived with her three children was indescribable. From early dawn they gathered near the airstrip all talking at once. Would the plane even arrive? What would the white-skinned young ones look like?

Finally, mid-morning, the cry went up. "Gununu! Gununu!" and the yellow Cessna came into sight over the tree-tops at the far end of the airstrip. As it taxied to a stop every eye was strained for a first glimpse. Then they just mobbed the plane, yodelling, exclaiming, shrieking with delight.

The Liddles' poor kiddies were not so delighted. As they took in the painted faces, and huge wigs, and the extent of the crowd, they cried out in fear. After a while we were able to quieten the crowd and explain the children's fears. They were immediately all concerned for them, and managed to stand back and be a little less boisterous. Eventually we moved away up the 800 metres of road to the houses. In no time at all the children lost their fear. I well remember young Geoff's face as he made his teddy-bear cry for a group of curious visitors and then laughed at them as they fearfully fled, thinking it was an evil spirit.

To Pori

January-July 1962

"Please, will you give me work?" Kay and Ivor looked doubtful as they faced the small, somewhat dishevelled eleven-year-old at the door. "Could you keep on working every day? Surely you will get tired after a few weeks? Then you will want to go back to your home and your carefree ways," said Ivor.

"No, Sir, I won't get lazy. Please, can I come and help you?"

"Can we trust you? Perhaps you will steal our things when we are away from the house?" Kay said to him.

"I will not steal!" he replied indignantly.

"Will you keep on doing as you are told?" Ivor challenged him.

"Yes, yes, I will do as you say. I will really look after you," he ended confidently.

Kay smiled to himself. "Perhaps," he thought aloud. "He has never known a moment's discipline. Taught to be cheeky to his mother, he has never been spanked, never worked if he felt like going over the mountains or dropping the job on hand to sleep. As for looking after us—he has never seen a breakable dish, never washed his hands properly until very recently, never heard of the type of clothes to wear."

"But,"...Ivor mused, "This could be of the Lord."

"Come back tomorrow morning," Kay said to him. "We will give you an answer then."

Young Pita was a Yuna. He spoke Huli too. His story went something like this. One day when a Government Patrol passed near his home he trotted along curiously beside the men. One of the policemen noticed him and asked him to carry for him. Pita took hold of the strap of the rucksack and it slipped through his fingers to the ground. He tried again. Lifting it upside-down he tried in vain to get it to his back. Standing there with his arm through the strap, he looked puzzled and beaten. The policemen laughed and helped him to get it on correctly. Gleefully he set out through the scrub with head high and chest stuck out. After a couple of days they were getting along splendidly – not that they could say a word to each other, but they managed. Then, by dint of sign and gesture, the policemen invited Pita to go home to Koroba with him. The metropolis of Koroba! Pita's heart jumped. Would he!

He arrived there with goggling eyes. "What tremendous houses!" he thought, as he sighted the three homes of the Patrol Officers built of rough bush material, and the half-dozen police huts. What was the shining stuff on the roof of the smaller house alongside? He had never heard of roofing-iron to catch drinking water; that had to be carried from a spring somewhere up in the hills. And the houses must be cold with all those big holes in the walls. He had never dreamt of wanting light inside or of having a doorway big enough for a man to walk through erect. That would let an enemy in too easily. Then he stood still, mouth agape, as he saw smoke coming out of a special 'road' up on top of the house!

That night he 'slept cold' for the first time. Instead of curling up in a ball beside a smoking fire, he was told to wrap up in a couple of blankets.

"What is that?" he queried when handed a bowl of rice the next morning. The others were eating it, so it must be food. Encouraged by hunger, he found it wasn't really too bad, though it didn't satisfy him. He missed the over-full feeling after the usual large pile of sweet potatoes. The water he was given to drink looked very dirty, then to his amazement he found it was hot. The policemen said, "Cup tea."

"Cup tea," he repeated after him. He was told to wash himself and wear a laplap (piece of cloth wrapped around the waist, tucked in, and preferably held securely by a wide belt). He tried, too, to comb his matted tight curls. These people certainly were strange, but he was willing to co-operate. Then he went outside and watched the police drilling, saw them milling logs, riding bicycles and doing a thousand-and-one unheard of things.

But gradually he settled. It wasn't too hard to adapt at the age of eleven. He had to carry water, cut firewood and help prepare food for the policemen.

One day two strange white men came to live in the old house up on the hill. He was told that they were not Government personnel but something else, called 'missionaries'. He watched them for a while, liking what he saw. All the time he was learning more of the trade language, Papua New Guinea Tok Pisin. Then one day he plucked up the courage to go and ask them for work. He would like to earn some money and get for himself some of the wonderful things he had seen – things like razor-blades, matches, knives and even clothes, though he still felt uncomfortable in them. Everyone else around Koroba was getting them, so he would too.

Kay and Ivor decided, after prayer, that they should take him on. So he washed their dishes, blackened the tea-towels and turned their clothes brown, especially the day he decided to boil them in an old rusty drum instead of the nice clean one he had been given.

It saved their valuable time, once he had grasped a little of how these strange white-skins lived, so he 'looked after them' while they were living in the old place on the Government station and, again after I arrived, he still helped me with the extra jobs that accompany primitive house-keeping.

Yuna men -
holding a bird of paradise;
in traditional dress.

Gradually too, he came to grasp a little of the strange things Ivor tried to teach him. He spoke to him continually of one called God, and His Son, Jesus. He was the great good Spirit, Pita learned, the One who made everything. This God loved everyone, but hated the bad things they did. Pita had never done anything seriously wrong, of course. He had never killed a man or stolen anything of consequence.

In time, Ivor realised that Pita was the Lord's choice for an interpreter for the advance into Yuna-land. With this in mind, he concentrated even more on teaching him the trade language and the basics of the Gospel. He used him constantly for interpreting into Huli while still at Koroba. As Bible stories were repeated over and over in the various preaching centres, he learned them thoroughly. Then, too, there were the long personal chats while walking from place to place.

※

Fully involved in the work at Koroba, Ivor still kept making trips into the Yuna valleys, keeping in touch with the people, beginning to teach them and always on the lookout for airstrip sites. How we looked forward to the time when we would be actually living among these Yuna people.

A choice was made of the two airstrip sites at Kelabo after the Field Superintendent of MAF had flown and checked them. Work commenced. Wangano, the chief headman, was most co-operative and did a grand job of supervision. At one time he somehow got hold of a pair of toy binoculars and told the men that he could see who was not working down the far end of the strip. Everyone worked extremely well.

Ray and Ruth Brown had been at Kelabo for some time, trying to work on the Yuna language. They were members of the Wycliffe Bible Translators. Unable to get permits to reside among the Yuna people, they had persuaded informants to come into

Koroba. It was not the best situation, but now, with the prospect of us moving to Kelabo too, they went on in, rejoicing that they would soon have company. Ivor made frequent trips down there, spending several days away each time, and then returned to the work at Koroba.

Without doubt, the Lord had led to the commencing of the airstrip at Kelabo, and the preaching had already been appreciated by the people. Yet somehow we did not feel sure about settling there. Now, with Eric and Marion Madsen due in a few weeks to take our place working with Kay and Gwen at Koroba, we waited on the Lord to give us clear assurance.

He didn't. More and more we felt drawn towards the Pori Valley. But, it was impossible to get an airstrip in there. We could walk in over the mountains and were quite prepared to live two days' walk away, but it would be impossible to get carriers to keep on bringing our supplies in that way. We had to have a supply of trading goods as payment for building materials and labour on the airstrip and house. We had to have bulk foodstuffs. We couldn't live as they did on little else than three to four kilograms of sweet potatoes a day.

One day, Hibuya and Ndago, Yuna headmen, from the Pori Valley, arrived at Koroba and sat wearily on the laundry floor.

"We have come to invite you to Pori," they said. "We have talked it over and all the headmen and all the people want you to come." Then triumphantly they added, "We have found an airstrip site." Ivor showed no enthusiasm, lest it should buoy up false hopes. They had no idea of how long four hundred and sixty metres was, or how steep a hillside was. Used all their lives to running up and down mountains, a slope too steep for a plane to land on would seem almost like flat ground to them.

However, he did agree to go over as soon as he could and have a look at it. The place they had found was just past the rest house at Ayuguali where Ivor and Kay had slept the first night ever in Yuna-land. A series of ridges ran down towards the Pori River, quite steep all the way and very steep closer to the river. Immediately behind, the mountains rose almost sheer. Ivor paced it out and had to tell them it was too short, and also too close to the mountains for the plane to get away after rising off the strip.

They just kept walking along across the ridges heading back up the valley. Then, Ivor says, for no apparent reason, he stopped on the crest of a ridge and said, "What about this one?"

Obviously, they had never thought of it either, but they started to tramp down the bamboo and scrub that was growing on it. Then Ivor paced it out. Yes, it was a possibility. He told them very guardedly that it might just be all right.

"Please burn the whole ridge off," he told them. "I will come back in a week or two and have a look at it again."

The ridge ran on a slight angle to the river. Immediately opposite across the river was a break in the mountains where another stream ran down to join the Pori River.

"It just might give enough clearance for approach and take-off," he thought.

When he returned to Koroba he spoke to Max Flavel again by radio and asked him if he would come in for a survey-flight. Max, always alert to such messages, came at the first opportunity. This time there was a spare seat on the plane and I was able to go too. What an experience! I thoroughly enjoyed it. It was a real thrill to get my first look at the Pori Valley. I knew we would soon be living there. Max flew around the area and up and down the ridge and finally said, "O.K., go ahead and make your airstrip. The clearance will be adequate for take-off, though we may have to reduce the uplift a bit in order to rise out of the valley."

So back Ivor went over the mountains again to give a final careful check and say "yes", or "no", to the expectant people. The helpful Government Officer lent him levels and a tape. As he walked down the ridge and reached the bottom his heart sank; the bottom forty-five metres were too steep to use. This had not been apparent before when the area was cleared. Now he turned around, saying nothing to the headmen who were watching his every expression, and began measuring the shortened length. Up, up, up, two hundred, three hundred, four hundred metres, and then right into the side of a seven-metre knoll. It was no use; this would make the overall gradient too steep; the regulation maximum was one in eight. But...perhaps...it could be shifted?

"Dig a hole here," he asked. Down and down they had to go until the levels were correct.

"Well," he said, "the strip will have to come right up to here and you will have to remove all this earth. Can you do it? It will take many men working every day for many moons. Can you keep your men at it and finish the job?"

There was a long time of discussion as the headmen summed up the possibilities realistically. Then they spoke up, "We want you to come. We will do it."

That was all. And they did, thirteen months' hard grind. But that is another story.

All this time the Lord had been giving clear indication from His Word, as we followed the course of our daily readings, that He wanted us at Pori. As we talked and prayed it over with the Liddles and others, there were no doubts left. The Madsens were settling in at Koroba, and the airstrip was progressing at Kelabo. The Browns were naturally disappointed that we would not be going there, but we were confident that the Lord would soon send someone else. It was not much longer before Ian and Aileen Armitage moved up from the Sepik to Kelabo.

※

"Come and look at this!" Ivor shouted from amidst the trunks and boxes late Monday afternoon. Leaving the half-kneaded bread, I rushed through the door and there, coming up the ridge from the road were one...two...three...fifty-eight Yuna come to take him home with them to set up a permanent mission station in the Pori Valley. What a thrill, and what a picture they made! Short, well-built men and boys, the mature fellows with wide wigs decorated with several colours of everlasting daisies, faces smeared with bright red or yellow paint, others evilly black with pig's fat and soot, and many with wide pig tusks through their noses.

They were very excited and very tired. The local Huli rallied around collecting enough food and firewood for them. We had only asked for twenty, but there was safety in numbers, they thought, when venturing into enemy territory. There was praise in our hearts and a lump in our throats as we greeted them. Their enthusiasm had to be seen to be believed.

At dawn the next morning, May 1st, 1962, the Yuna advance was on. The carriers away, Ivor stopped for breakfast, then Kay took him five kilometres by motor-bike to join them at Koroba Government station.

It was only half-an-hour's walk to catch up with the carrier line, resting in a garden before they began crossing the swamp. They didn't like the mud, and wasted time trying to scramble around it rather than plough through it. So did Ivor. And then there were mountains – it was quite a job keeping up their morale. Most of them were pretty inexperienced as carriers. Leaders Hibuya and Ngado were worth their salt, and helped with carrying the most awkward items. Being taller, Ivor needed to lift some things himself in order to get them through the narrow grooved tracks in the soft limestone, holding some items at arm's length above his head.

Once they got to the top, he went ahead to the rest house and called out for the people to bring in food for the hungry men. The last weary fellow struggled in, in heavy rain, at 4:30 p.m. More men had come to meet them, swelling the number to seventy. The houses were full. Two men who had carried for Kay and Ivor on their initial trek treated Ivor like a long lost brother.

They were up with the birds in the morning. The carriers got away by half-past six. More and more kept arriving to help. When they arrived at the mission station site, dozens more people gathered. The tent was pitched, a cook-house built and everything packed into the small space two and a half metres by three and a half, by half-past three, just as the rain began to pour down. Ivor promised to pay the carriers the next day. Everyone wanted to start work on the house; they had chosen the site themselves and had some timber already in place. Though the tent was leak-proof, it certainly wasn't mosquito-proof. Ivor complained, "They nearly carried me away, they were so many and so big. Net up—big sleep!"

Men crowded in soon after dawn and pressed around Ivor until he could get handles into the spades for them to start levelling the house site. After sorting out trade items for paying the carriers, he was just ready to start when the plane came over for an airdrop of goods. What a crowning boost to the already evident enthusiasm. There was a 100% recovery of the airdrop, although the drop-site had not been cleared of sticks and stumps and stones. The flight had not been expected for another two days.

Eventually Ivor got everyone lined up again and gave them a talk about pay before starting to give it out. He told them that there would be much more for work on the house and airstrip. They were obviously very satisfied with what they got, and said, "We'll go again anytime. Our hearts are happy," and other comments of the sort. It seemed that the most coveted item of pay was a mirror – which pandered to their vanity!

It took a day or two to get the various clan groups organised into different jobs – one helping on the house, another clearing top-soil half-way down the strip, a third starting to remove the mountain at the top end of the strip. It was a hectic round, everybody needed constant supervision – they had, for example, to be shown which way up to hold a spade. Endless talking, everybody boss! They were so very keen to get going; everyone wanted to help, but didn't really know how.

On Sunday morning about a hundred people came to the little service on the cleared house-site. Ivor had explained the day before that this would be a day when there would be no work. Some were influenced by the rumours that had been put around that he would forbid the eating of pork. He had a long talk about it and Pita confirmed that he had eaten bacon for breakfast, hoping that they would talk to those who had stayed away because of it. A rumour no doubt started by some who wished us out of the valley. The women were fearful of sickness, the reprisals of evil spirits, or beatings if they attended, so none came.

What a swarm of blowflies there were. With bodies smeared with pig fat and never washed…enough said and, to add to it all, Ivor cooked cabbage for lunch. A thunderstorm in the early afternoon sent everyone home, and it was good to have quiet to rest, meditate and pray, without the pressure of enthusiastic crowds.

※

Yes, Satan's domain had been entered, but he had no intention of giving ground without waging war. There were some blood-chilling experiences in those early days, not so much of physical danger as of spiritual, with the consciousness of the nearness of real evil powers.

A week later Ivor wrote to me:

Ayuguali.

Sunday, 13th May, 1962.

"My Dear Marjorie,

Sunday is almost gone. I have just opened three tins of food. Peas and sausages to eat with the inevitable sweet potatoes, and a tin of apricots for dessert. Today has been the quietest of my experiences in Yuna-land.

"After the all-out efforts of the week and some experiences hard to take, I had a good sleep-in this morning. There was still ample time for preparation of heart and message before the service. At the beginning, lots of boys, a few men, and some old men gathered. I was especially happy to see the old chaps. Will they be with us long enough to understand and turn their hardened old hearts to the Saviour?

"Some women walked past down the hill and I had the interpreter call out a welcome to them, but they were too fearful. I could only continue with the service. I was teaching the basics of the character and power of God through the story of Creation.

"Half-way through, a group of women and a few girls returned. I was able to persuade the men to move together and make room for them to sit down within hearing distance. They came ever so timidly, but sat down and listened enthralled. The first Yuna women to hear. I prayed the Lord's protection for them as any sickness or accident would be interpreted as a reprisal of the spirits for their having come.

"Soon after lunch, I was lying down reading when I heard the death wail close by. After a quick prayer I grabbed the medical kit and rushed outside. As I approached a group of women just across the gardens, they moved away in fear, all except the mother who was sitting cross-legged with the sick one on her knees. A tiny baby. It took me some time to be sure it was actually dead. How I wished you had been here.

"The wailing stopped when I arrived. I wonder if the mother secretly hoped that this white man might have some mystical power to give her baby back to her again? But all I could offer was a heart of sympathy, and that only by look and gesture and a few confused phrases. My heart was touched and I wondered how I would feel if it was my child.

"I haven't yet heard whether she was at the meeting this morning. I could wish not, I suppose. She is one of Hibuya's wives, the headman who came in to Koroba to invite us over here. He has been such a nice chap to deal with. I hope this will not affect him adversely.

"Another little life has gone to be with the Lord. There must be a lot of Yuna in Heaven with Him now. I hate to think of how many have gone the other way, without hearing of their Saviour. May there be many who turn to Him soon through our ministry here. This is my prayer and longing."

Three days later Ivor continued the letter:

"Hibuya came in today and I had a chat with him about the baby's death. He said, 'Up until now we have only known the fashion of pig killing for healing. Now, when my children are ill, I want them to come to you for prayer and medicine.' I explained to him that the baby had gone to God's good land where he will be happy and well cared for, and pointed out that if he and his wife hear the teaching that we give them, and believe in God, they too will go to God's good land and see their little one again. As I spoke his face lit up into a pleasant smile. He has been to only one meeting so far, yet there was something really responsive there.

"I'm sorry to have to report that the carriers took two full days to get back with the food. Thanks for the letters. It was a tonic to hear from you and other loved ones again. The bread was nice and I waded through some of the meat. I curried the mutton and ate some of it. The stew was somewhat better, but disappointing – it looked beautiful in the jar. Don't try again, just send bacon. One of the boxes of mirrors was shattered, too.

"Just on dark, Wednesday night, a call came from down the hill that they could see an evil spirit above my tent. Pita was scared stiff. Choking back the tears, he came to ask, pleadingly, if he could go and sleep with friends, so of course I sent him off.

That night I cried to the Lord over and over again as I felt the chill of Satanic evil. I cast myself on Him asking in His name for relief from the pressure of it. The word of God was a great comfort to my heart. But I knew the reality of, 'Our struggle is not against flesh and blood but against the powers…'

"The next night, just as I got in from work about 6 p.m., a shout went up, followed by a roar like the approach of a jet plane. I rushed outside to see my cook-house in full flames. The bamboo around it must have exploded all at once. My tent was walled around with bamboo to keep the wind out and it was alight too. Six of us worked like men possessed tearing out the bamboo, and pouring water on the tent-fly, but minutes later, with eyes bloodshot with smoke and tears, I estimated the damage at 35 Australian pounds (about Kina 2,000 today) and the inconvenience—well!

"Almost dark, the tent-fly ruined, large holes smouldering all over the new tent. As it was rubberised we had to cut around the patches that were all right. It seemed like tragedy! Though all personal effects and trade goods and gear were undamaged, they were exposed to the threatening thunderstorm.

"Men and boys turned up from all angles. One old chap threw his arms around me in sympathy. It was the first such demonstration I have seen here. It meant so much. A moment's pondering told me we had to cover the stuff where it was. We started a little house, but the moon was up and we were barely under way when we realised that it was impossible. Then Hibuya came up with the answer. Boys ran off to get banana leaves while the men built a shaky frame over the top of the tent. With the leaves spread on top, and a wall of bamboo around the sides, the task was completed. The Lord withheld the storm and, although a light rain fell, not a drop penetrated.

"It was later, when we were sitting around the remains of the cook-house, that the story was pieced together. There was much excited talking. I realised that they were blaming the fire on the rama (evil spirit) that they had seen the night before. I thought of Job. The Lord gave Satan power to destroy all his property, possessions and family. Many thoughts came to mind and then the Lord made clear to me what He would have me to say.

" 'Truly,' I said, 'Satan, the headman, and all his rama are resisting my coming here. They know that all the Yuna who listen to God's talk and take on His fashion, will be liberated. They will not be afraid of the rama any more, but will be happy people with God's blessing. But God is greater than Satan. He will enable us to win His battles, and He will bring deliverance to you and your people through Jesus.'

"There was quite a bit of talk, then both Hibuya and Ngado said, 'Yes, that is right. We want to learn about God's fashion. Please pray to God to protect us when we are working in the bush. The spirits that live in the trees may harm us when we are felling them for your house.'

"So my heart was full of praise to God. I willingly laid down the spoiling of my goods at His feet, since it brought such thoughts and decisions to these primitive people so early on. Later I read Joshua 3:5, 'Consecrate yourselves, for tomorrow the Lord will do amazing things among you,' and verse 7, 'I am with you as I was with Moses'. I was conscious of His presence and convinced by His words. Then I turned to The Reaper Bible Class notes for the day, and it was headed 'Sure to be kept.' Hallelujah!

"After everyone had left me, I was having a bit of a wash outside, with the little lamp pegged on to the clothes line. With joy in my heart over the attitude of the folk were taking, I was singing lustily, when I became conscious of a voice calling from down the hill. It was Pita asking what I had said. So at the top of my voice I called back, 'Mi amamas, God i no lusim mi, Em i lukautim mi.' (I am happy. God has not forsaken me. He is looking after me.)

"Ten minutes later he appeared at the door. With him were two other youngsters, all scared stiff, with their eyes nearly popping out. They said, 'You said that God had forsaken you, and a man (to them an evil spirit) was fighting with you. We came to help you. You are only one. We could not leave you unaided.' Certainly it is all tremendously real to them. Won't it be wonderful to be able to say soon, 'He breaks the power of cancelled sin, He sets the prisoner free.'!

"The next morning the people flocked in to help me build a house. Women turned up in numbers with thatching grass and everyone worked showing a friendly, sympathetic attitude that was a thrill to experience. If the spirits had been at me, then they knew what that was like. By mid-afternoon the job was completed and all the gear shifted in, just in time for folk to get home before the rain poured down.

"So the difficult experiences become joyous ones. When Satan oversteps the mark, God turns it to His glory and His work goes ahead. I have chosen eight small Yuna boys to go back with the carriers to attend the Koroba Boarding School, for an English education. Each has his parents' consent and the approval of the leaders of his respective clan. The kids are thrilled with the adventure of it all. Some of them have never been out of the Pori Valley! I was interested to see Mbaluba, tough fight leader, put his arms around them and cuddle them, at the same time giving them a great old lecture on how to behave. Pray for them, and give this list of their names to Kay so that he can contact them when he takes Religious Instruction at the school. The years will tell their own story as to whether they grow up in the Lord and become useful to Him as Bible translators or teachers of the Word.

"Please share this news and pass on my regards to all at Koroba.

Lovingly,

Ivor."

The weeks sped by. Ivor was fully occupied supervising several gangs of inexperienced fellows at once. One gang on the airstrip, one on the house, one out in the bush felling timber, another preparing ground for a garden, others working tracks, or cutting grass with a long knife. Then, too, there were daily meetings as well as the Sunday services. Most valuable of all were the continual contacts as problems and attitudes were discussed, and an insight into their customs and culture was gradually gained.

One man who had not been very friendly decided after a chat to go along with us, and promised help to build chapels in his part of the valley. Another good contact was made with a group by going duck-shooting with them one Saturday afternoon. They had a hilarious time trying to get out onto the lake on improvised rafts, but failed to retrieve the wounded duck that they were after. The big thing was that they were so very friendly from then on.

Another good means of gaining friends was by removing their rotten, painful teeth. There were many of them coming, often several a day, once the word spread that it could be done with a special iron gadget in a matter of seconds. It was done without anaesthetic, but the pain was nothing compared to what they endured by their own method. The victim sat down and held his head in one hand, in the other he held a sharpened stick against the offending molar. A kind friend tapped away at the other end of the stick with a stone, and it could take up to three days before the tooth was broken away enough to end the torture. Even then they sometimes failed to get the nerve, and the stump which they were then unable to do anything about, continued to give them pain. So it was not unusual for a man to jump up and grab Ivor's hand, or throw his arms around him, exclaiming delightedly that the thing was out!

God's laws and ways were taught through the things that happened from day to day, such as wife-beating, adultery, a man taking a fourth or fifth wife, a lad claiming he had never sinned, a father laughing at his son's insolence. In a communal society everyone listens to everything that is said, with no such thing as privacy. So a point goes home to many ears and hearts each time a matter is raised.

It was nearing time for the Annual Conference. A whole year had gone by since the decision had been made to move into the Highlands and now it was time to get together again at Anguganak for the wonderful fellowship, the discussion of problems and methods of working, and the ministry of some visiting teacher of the Word. The Conference gave happy times of chit-chat together, fun and laughter, too, and a sharing of some of the things that got on top of one when isolated in the bush, things which fell back into perspective when discussed with someone else who had had the same experiences.

So Ivor packed up. One morning, still in the dark, holding a kerosene pressure-lantern to light the way, he left Pori for Kelabo. He faced ten hours of tough mountain walking, but it was necessary to see what progress was being made on the airstrip down there. He spent a few days encouraging, instructing and preaching, and then came on in to Koroba. How good it was to be back together again.

A few days later came an eventful trip out to Anguganak. MAF pilot Harold Morton picked us up one very foggy morning, and with Eric Madsen in the front seat we set course direct for Anguganak. I say 'set course', but before very long we were here, there, and everywhere, dodging banks of heavy cloud. We had just cleared the central ranges when all of a sudden Harold put the plane into a steep dive. Poor Eric got a real fright. He was quietly writing a letter at the time. We were a little more used to flying high in tiny Cessnas, but it was still a shock as the machine back-fired loudly several times in rapid succession.

As we topped the last range, Harold had only a moment to decide whether to go under or over the tremendous cloud bank that was covering the entire Sepik Plains. We went under; down and down, until we were flying at tree-top level, watching the startled birds below us and the clouds immediately above us. On and on, until we thought we must be almost at Anguganak. The radio crackled and we heard Colin Cliffe's voice, "Bravo Victor Romeo," he called to Harold, "I can hear you a little to the north of Anguganak. Now you are right overhead. There is a small break in the clouds a hundred metres off the end of the strip. Can you make it?"

Round and round, round and round we circled with the clouds now below us as well as above and knowing that close by was the 500-metre Anguganak bluff.

"No," Harold called back to Colin on the ground, "I can't

make it. We will have to head north to the coast and then out to Wewak."

So we stretched our cramped legs as best we could and settled down for a third hour. Late in the afternoon we took off again and this time made it in to Anguganak All the fellowship and fun was more than worth it.

Conference over, Ivor returned to Koroba to walk back into Pori and get a bit further along with the house, while I remained at Anguganak for a month's medical course, held by Dr. John Sturt. I had not been well for a while and could not have managed the walk in to Pori at that stage. By the end of the month, I was fit, and impatient to get back to Koroba, and packed-up and away.

Ivor came in from Pori a couple of days ahead of me. Together we packed up our remaining possessions, spring-cleaned the house for the Madsens to move into, sent word for our carriers, and waited.

Waited, because they did not come to get us; that was not the day that we had arranged. However, two days later, late in the afternoon, there they were. It looked like a whole army coming up the ridge from the road. They had come all right, dozens of them. Once they were housed and fed, Ivor and his brother Neville set to work to prepare some extra loads of gear. It was midnight when they finished.

The next morning the raucous alarm clock woke us suddenly, "Br.r.r.r.r," I cried back. "It's dark and cold yet!" Pulling the blankets over my ear I went to snuggle down again, but then in an instant I was wide awake. This was the day we had prayed for, and waited for, for months.

Today was the day...My sluggish mind began to remember... "Today we are to set off for Pori together...There are last-minute things to pack, carriers to start, mountains to cross, and the Pori mission station to set up – the first among the Yuna tribe."

"Carriers are ready for a dawn start," Ivor's voice floated back to me as the wind slammed the front door for him. I was already rolling up the mattresses. It was light now inside the wee thatch-and-bamboo shack. Here in the tropics dawn came suddenly with only fifteen minutes from bird-call until it was light enough to read.

"He e e e e wa, he e e e ewa," – a crescendo yodelling penetrated the mist-filled valley. Rushing outside to the far side of the house section, I looked over the bank down on to the red clay road. More than a hundred and fifty men and boys were snaking along, single filed, half running to keep warm. Even at only 5 degrees south of the equator, it was cold at 1,700 metres altitude.

Red and green flour drums strapped on to broad backs held an assortment of clothes, bedding, books, kitchen ware, trade goods and food stuffs, often mixed together to give the required weight of 16 kilograms. Others carried boxes, cartons or packages on their heads or shoulders, or in large string bags on their backs. Swinging from a stick between two muscular pairs of shoulders were two dozen bright red spade heads.

"Misisi," an urgent voice called from outside the back door. Ivor had sent four youths to get the mattresses, lunch, medical kit and raincoats that were to be kept with us along the way. What a sight they made. Fuzzy, never washed hair, formed into huge wigs and decorated with bright yellow dried daisies; white eyes and teeth, contrasting sharply with faces blackened with pig's fat and soot; and a pig's tusk pushed through the nasal septum and turned downwards, making them look really fierce. Each was carrying a string bag on his back with the ends knotted in the front of one shoulder, and had circlets of string surrounding his hips holding a sporran in front and a bunch of leaves behind.

"Harago, harago!" (hurry up) one called impatiently as I filled the thermos flask with coffee. They were in a hurry. Shivering but strong arms collected up the bundles and, with a whoop and an ear-splitting yodel, they too were off.

Ivor and Neville were coming back up the ridge. Geoff Liddle arrived at the back door along with them, "Breakfast's ready," he announced. After Gwen had heaped our plates with energy for the day, Kay read to us from Living Gospels, Mark 16:15, *"Go throughout the whole world and preach the gospel to all people"*. Then, turning to Mathew 28:20, he added, *"And surely I am with you always"*.

Feelingly, he commended us, the future, and especially the Yuna, to the Lord.

Five kilometres by motor-cycle brought us to the Government station. "What a line of carriers!" Mr. Hayward exclaimed. "I thought it was a dawn attack on the station!" He looked as though he was still recovering from shock.

"It just seemed as though no one wanted to be left behind," Ivor explained. "I asked for fifty, thinking they would be plenty, but last night we counted in one hundred and sixty-eight. However, they can change around, spelling each other and sharing the loads. They will have to share the pay, too, of course."

We chatted for a few minutes, collected a few plants and cuttings, then with his reassurance of help at any time, we were off. Off the road, our first obstacle was a deep stinking swamp contaminated by pig's droppings and human filth. It was crisscrossed with wide drains, often with up to a metre of mud in the bottom. But as I approached each one, two boys rushed past me with a plank, five metres by forty-five centimetres, and laid it across the top. Such instant bridging saved me many a scramble down, through, and up out again.

I stepped out confidently onto a firm looking clump of grass. "Whoops!" I cried in amazement, "It's moving!"

"Yes it's floating grass," my experienced partner informed me as he jumped expertly from one clump to the next. "Keep moving," he called over his shoulder. "It might sink if you linger." I did keep moving and an hour later we emerged onto higher, firmer ground.

The mountains towered immediately in front of us. Passing through bush filled with bird song we came, in a few minutes, on to a little cleared knoll. All the Koroba Valley lay before us, sun-drenched and sparkling. Little patches of fog lingered in a few sheltered hollows, as though reluctant to leave. Here and there a curl of smoke indicated the presence of a house. Women and children were moving out to their gardens for the day's work. Lush green in the distance was yet another swamp, while all was encircled by a backdrop of high blue mountains. Ivor was humming to himself, and I joined in with the words:

When through the woods and forest glades I wander,
And hear the birds sing sweetly in the trees,
When I look down from lofty mountains' grandeur,
And hear the brook, and feel the gentle breeze,
    Then sings my soul, my Saviour God, to Thee,
    How great Thou art, how great Thou art.
And when I think that God, His Son not sparing,
Sent Him to die, I scarce can take it in.
That on the cross, my burden gladly bearing,
He bled and died to take away my sin,
    Then sings my soul, my Saviour God, to Thee,
    How great Thou art, how great Thou art.

We stood drinking in such beauty that our hearts glowed with joy and gratitude to our God. How could it be that He had chosen us, and brought us here high up in the mountains in the heart of Papua New Guinea, to bring the Gospel to people who had never heard of Jesus Christ?

We moved on. Up, and up, and up we went and then down a little, and up, and up again. In places we crossed steep limestone ridges with only an old root to cling to. Sometimes if the step was too high or slippery, Ivor reached down a helping hand and lifted me up bodily. In some places, with the washing of heavy rain and constant pad, pad of many feet, the soft limestone was worn down to the narrowest of tracks. Care had to be taken not to kick one's ankle with the boot on the other foot. The bush was beautiful with ferns, rhododendrons, coloured creepers and orchids. "If only I could lift my eyes off the tangle of roots and vines and enjoy it," I thought.

A few minutes later I was up above the roots and vines and balancing along the trunk of a fallen giant. Suddenly I was sitting in the mud way down below nursing a painful ankle. Ivor scrambled down to help me up and after a few steps I was able to walk on it again. We ploughed along through the mud, unable to remount the tree. The word was shouted forward along the line of carriers that 'Misisi' had fallen and that her 'trousisi' were now caked with mud.

Finally at 2,100 metres, we dropped down on a small grassy clearing. A thoughtful boy handed me a gourd of water. Then, "cup tea ti kua," – Ivor's voice floated down the line of carriers to the one who had the lunch. He sat down by me with a packet of sandwiches and a flask of piping hot coffee.

After lunch we snatched five minutes' more rest, then it was, "Come on, up you get. I want to get you there before the afternoon rain starts." Down and up, down and up, until finally it was just down, literally just down as we descended the mountain by a ladder of logs. Nor did we keep ahead of the rain. It poured down, rushing past us, down our necks and in and out of our boots. The logs were slippery and I steadied my trembling knees with a hand on Ivor's shoulder below and in front of me. As he encouraged with the words, "Look, you are in the Pori Valley!". My heart leapt. Here we were at last, into yet another sphere of service into which the Lord had clearly led.

A few minutes later, we reached the Guranda 'rest house' and the first of the two days' journey was over. What a relief to pull off those muddy boots and wet socks and to have a bath. That is if a bucket of water in a crude roofless shelter, with light rain falling, is a bath. Then after chatting with the folk who gathered around, and buying food for the men who were with us, we ate a meal of bully beef and tinned mixed vegetables and gratefully stretched out tired limbs on canvas stretchers set up on the dirt floor.

That first night in the Pori Valley was not a very pleasant one. It was cold and rather eerie. There had been an argument among the carriers and a near fight over the food we had bought for them. Watching their faces as they argued, I realised just how fiery and quick-tempered they were. We had filled a vacuum flask at tea time so now at 1 a.m. I got up for a hot drink and hotty.

The next morning most of the carriers were away by 7.30 a.m. We lingered a while, chatting with the people of the place, and got away about nine o'clock, with the few fellows we had kept to carry things that we might need along the way. Cresting a small knoll, we startled a lone woman and her two toddlers working in a garden. The kiddies shrieked and the three of them fled in terror at the sight of a white woman. I called and called to her, and the men with us laughed at her, but I could still hear the kiddies crying as we moved on. Further along, one woman was waiting at the side of the road and presented me with a stick of sugar cane, a token of welcome and friendship.

She was wearing only a grass skirt hanging from below a distended abdomen, and tied tightly around her hips. It hung to just above the knees and completely surrounded her body except for a small gap either side. Her hair was in tight curls, cropped short. A large string bag with the ends knotted in front of her forehead hung down to hip level at the back.

A number of men spoke to us as we passed by their gardens. Most had huge wigs decorated colourfully with bird feathers or dried flowers. They wore a string sporran in front and a large bunch of fresh leaves at the back, held by several circlets of string. Through his belt each carried a stone axe and in his hand a two metre bow with a bundle of arrows.

"I haven't noticed many houses," I said to Ivor later in the day.

"No," he replied. "They are well hidden away for fear of

enemies. Many of the folk who garden here during the day return across the river and up into the mountains at night." Pointing to a hollow behind a garden he said, "There is a house down there. See it?"

"No, I can't," I replied straining my eyes, unable to recognise anything as a house.

"Look through between the banana palms. Can't you see the blackened thatch?" And so it was. Only an experienced eye could have picked it out. Two metres high, it merged almost indiscernibly into the bank behind it and the garden around it.

During the early afternoon the clouds banked up, and down came the rain, but we had to press on; there was no time or place to shelter. As we descended the valley, it gradually widened out, but without any flat ground. We pushed our way through patches of bush or scrub and bamboo, where old gardens had been left to revert and renew. In some areas there were acres of coarse kunai grass, but much of the valley was sweet potato gardens.

These gardens consisted of hundreds of mounds 30 centimetres high and up to a metre across, covered with dark green runners. Some were freshly planted, others needed weeding of the kunai grass that grows so quickly. Many more were in various stages of preparation. The sweet potato takes seven to nine months to mature and the people must keep up a continuous supply for themselves, their children, and their pigs.

Clumps of bananas and pandanas nut trees were planted in sheltered hollows and I began to detect a few more houses in such corners. Muddy hollows were planted with taro, or reeds for making grass skirts.

Most apparent were the burial boxes. There were many of them, far, far, too many, standing out because they were put on a knoll and surrounded by bright red crotons. Adult boxes were over a metre long, placed up on stakes a little over a metre above the ground. Most were covered with a few planks or a bit of thatching.

Carriers on the way to Pori.

Thatching the first missionary house.

So we continued on our way down the Pori Valley. We could hear, but not see, the river in a deep gorge on our right side. Mountains up to 3000 metres towered behind it. We were descending to 1500 metres as we approached the site of the Pori Mission Station.

When we were nearly home the rain ceased temporarily, and the whole party assembled under a clump of pine trees. Ivor looked at me and said, "You need a cup of coffee." Mbaluba's face was a study when he saw what Ivor was doing. Irritated, incredulous, tolerant and amused, I watched the parade of emotions. Fighting chief and husband of four wives, ruler of all he surveyed, he had never in his wildest dreams been considerate of anyone, let alone a woman.

Ten minutes later, on the way again, the rain descended in a downpour such as is experienced only in the tropics. All the local people had long since taken refuge in their houses to blow up the fire and warm their bare, wet bodies. As we passed close to their house, Mbaluba's two teenage wives appeared, shivering, shy, somewhat fearful. Just what was a white woman? – a demon? a witch? But as I smiled and called to them in their own language Mbaluba led me over to them. He laughed at their fears, making comments which, no doubt, I was better off not understanding.

Finally, Gebogone raised her big brown eyes to my face, and rubbing her wrists up and down over her bare breasts exclaimed, "Ah. oo.oo, ah.oo.oo.," over and over again. I turned to greet Baminya standing behind her. Speechless with fear and excitement, she chewed on the bent knuckle of her forefinger and retired backwards, giggling, into the bushes.

They disappeared into their houses and we continued the last four hundred metres into our half-built home at 4 p.m. Because of the tremendous rain there was no welcoming party – only the exhausted carriers stood shivering dejectedly in a semi-circle behind the cargo. Ivor quickly sent them all home, promising them their pay in two days' time.

An inspection of the loads of gear revealed a few damp books and a gluey mass in the top of the drum of flour, but no real damage. So happy to be here, Ivor took me in his arms and thanked God for His enabling for the journey now behind us, and for the days immediately ahead. Mattresses were soon unrolled on the floor, and a couple of tins of food opened, then to bed and sleep.

I really enjoyed that walk, experiencing the Lord's literal undertaking physically. It was two seven-hour days, over virtually trackless billows of mountains. The Lord gave not only endurance but joy, and no stiff muscles the next day – just another incident where He provided abundantly more than we asked for.

Most of the next day was spent opening the sixteen kilogram loads of gear, drying damp articles and repacking them, for we had nowhere else to put anything. Every few minutes we paused to exchange greetings with the Yuna tribesmen who came to stare at the white woman. Some wanted to sell us sweet potatoes or corn cobs, pumpkins or a type of coarse cabbage.

The house was still just a shell. The floor was split palm, each piece being rounded and springy to walk on. Only half of it was down. The walls were made of sheets of bamboo, flattened out and then woven, and only the outside ones were up as yet. There were no windows or doors, not even outside ones. Ivor tied some strips of old canvas over the lounge window holes and put window-like shutters in the bedroom—these let some light in but couldn't be seen through.

The garden that Ivor had planted a couple of months before was well up, and promising a bumper crop of Western vegetables.

We only slept in the house, and worked towards getting it liveable. Outside was the hut that had been built the day after the tent was burnt. In there we stored everything on the dirt floor and had a low camping table for meals. Then fourteen metres further away was a small cook-house, with just an open fire and half a two hundred litre drum for the stove. Three holes were cut in the bottom (which was now the top) just like a regular stove. A pressure cooker was a wonderful boon; I even cooked bread in it. First of all, the bread was set in a bowl and placed on top of a kerosene tin with a small kerosene wick lamp burning underneath for warmth. For cooking it, I took the ring out of the pressure cooker. While the bottom of the loaf was cooking, the top continued to rise, of course, but when it was turned, it came back to a reasonable shape and made a nice loaf.

Until our garden reached production, we used quite a lot of tinned foods along with the daily sweet potatoes, corn and cabbage, brought in to us by the people. The Koroba missionaries were visited weekly by MAF, and we had our mail and groceries brought in to there most weeks. Sometimes we got butter or bacon; more often, we used tinned margarine and, of course, there was no fresh meat.

After a while we had six pullets carried over the mountains. Fed on local foods with a little meatmeal, they gave us plenty of eggs and an occasional roast dinner. Many of the people had never seen poultry before and they used to stand outside the run poking blades of grass in for them to peck at.

We even had a couple of kittens brought in when the rats got too ravenous. What a joke it was to see Mbaluba, fighting chief and powerful leader, standing for an hour pulling a piece of string for the kittens to play with!

I suppose, looking back, that conditions were pretty primitive in those early days. We were not aware of it at the time, nor could we have been happier together in the centre of God's will. What more could a Christian desire?

Marjorie and Ivor at work outside their thatched house

Ivor in discussion with Yuna elder

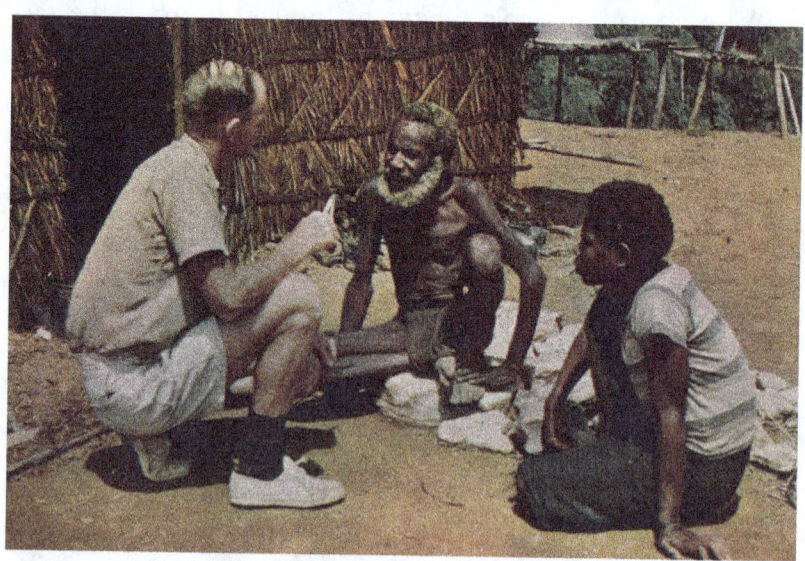

3

A WORK BEGINS

Keep your roots deep in him, build Your lives on him, and become stronger in your faith.

Colossians 2:7 (GNB)

Murder!

The distraught woman screamed incoherently at me as she appeared over the brow of the hill. I looked up startled, somewhat fearful too, for I was away from the house, working alone down in the garden. It was just two days since we had walked into Pori together. Ivor came running and intercepted her. I tried to understand what she was telling us in Huli, but she was so upset that I could not get a word. Pita appeared on the scene and managed to get her story.

Her daughter, she said, had been working in the garden near a patch of bush while she herself had gone away for something. When she came back she called the 16-year-old girl without response. Searching around she came across her battered body in the hollow just inside the bush, so she came rushing to us just ten minutes away.

There was nothing we could do, other than show her that we were sorry, and she soon rushed off again, calling out to all and telling them what had happened.

The next morning a group of the leaders came to talk about it. They were after the culprit's blood and Ivor had a hard job to convince them that they must not kill him, but take him to Koroba and hand him over to the Government for trial.

In the afternoon a group of them came back saying that they knew who the murderer was. They were still determined to kill him themselves. Again Ivor spoke to them very sternly indeed and they said, "All right, we will bring him here to your house, and you can see us kill him." They seemed to mean, "Then you can tell the Government that you saw us do it and that we did it properly."

Finally, Ivor prevailed, and they agreed not to make blood run, but to go ahead and capture him without harming him.

An hour later they returned with a seventeen-year-old lad. Our hearts nearly broke as we looked at his downcast young face. Instead of a cruel hardened criminal, he seemed such a nice youngster, and we almost wept. The accusers were sure of him, though he pleaded "not guilty".

Towards dusk they all started drifting away. Finally, Ivor questioned them about arrangements for the night and they replied that he could stay with us. "Can't he sleep in the cookhouse with Pita?" they wanted to know. Pita's eyes jumped out like organ stops and his face went as white as a brown one can. It took more stern talking to make the headman accept his responsibilities.

On Sunday morning we waited a long time for folk to gather for the service. Later we learned that there was a big gathering at the girl's graveside. We asked if they would like us to go too. They seemed delighted, so I grabbed a snack to take with us and we set off.

Tiaga, the Government-trained medical man, walked beside us to explain things, interpret for us and help in any way necessary. All the clans from nearby were gathered to give pig meat as a gesture of sympathy, and the murderer's clan were to pay the first instalment of the compensation.

The first indication of activity was the sound of women wailing. Then as we crested the brow of a kunai ridge, we spied a large group of men in close formation rushing about, making a tremendous noise. Coming closer we asked permission to take a photo of them. All were carrying two and a half metre spears, axes, or bows and arrows. Some had sides of freshly killed pig over their shoulders. They were charging about in columns in their clan groups yodelling, yelling and obviously enjoying it to the full. It could quite easily have been most frightening, but through the pig fat, soot, red clay and other decorations we could pick out faces we knew—faces of men who had carried our goods from Koroba, and faces of fellows who had been working on the airstrip or house.

They beamed a welcome at us, being just thrilled that the white people had come.

Now we could see large groups of women, some crying, some laughing, some dancing little ditties, all moving slowly towards the burial ground. When they realised I was there, they mobbed me, calling out, "Sister, sister, white sister." I was able to converse a little with those who were Huli bi-linguals. They reached out their filthy finger-nails to scratch my white skin to see if it was lime that would come off!

Up the hill, the men, still in their clan groups, were butchering the sides of a pig. Some were still to be slaughtered. While one man held the pig in his arms another struck it on the head with a club. Then they were placed on the fire to singe the bristles. Using razor-sharp bamboo knives, they were cut according to a definite system. As the bamboo became blunt, it was quickly resharpened by removing a slither with the teeth. Mostly they cut better than the steel knives that we had given out for pay. Four dozen pigs were cut up.

While Ivor and Tiaga were watching the men, I got caught up in the large group of women moving towards the elevated grave site two hundred yards down the hill. Three hundred women closed in, chanting, dancing wildly and weeping, some genuinely, others just joining in the sorrow. All were pregnant with fear—fear of evil spirits and fear of the departed spirit. Though encircled, I could see over their heads, as they were not tall. Yuna men averaged 163 cms and the women were proportionally shorter.

A few women were right by the coffin, banging on it with special black sticks and crying frantically to the spirits. They had taken the top off the box. Then the mother led me by the hand to look in. It was not a lovely scene, a decomposing body that had been battered with a fence paling, hordes of blowflies, surrounded by the distorted faces of women calling out to the evil spirits. Then Tiaga and Ivor joined us. Tiaga was able to quieten the women down and Ivor told them a little about God, and expressed special sympathy for the mother. He encouraged them to come and hear God's talk so that when they died they could go to God's good place and be happy, free of the spirits.

Later, up on a little knoll, we looked down on the scene. A long fire was burning, heating the lumps of limestone for cooking the meat. Every few minutes a stone would explode and there would be loud cries as folk fled from the flying fragments. There were seven or eight hundred people milling around.

When all the groups of men, all armed, gathered in a large circle the tension was electric. This was the final harangue to decide what compensation the murderer's clan should pay to those who were bereaved. In the centre of the circle lay two dozen halves of pig meat. Mbaluba, the fighting chief and headman, was in the centre with the dead girl's father. There was some arguing and some threats, and then Mbaluba's voice boomed out, "The missionary is here," he said. "He has come to teach a better way than the fighting way. The Government too has told us to stop fighting or pay the consequences. We are not going to fight."

He glared around the group, daring anyone to defy him. Finally, the girl's father made a gesture indicating that he would accept the decision. The dead girl's clan picked up the meat from the centre of the circle and all moved off to continue enjoying the celebrations.

The extra meat was hurriedly added to that already prepared for the pit oven. Down in the grass a little way away, the women were cleaning the intestines. Later some of them would be given portions of the cooked meat too.

Now the stones were hot, the pit dug and all the food ready to go in; first a layer of hot stones, then a covering of broad leaves; then the meat and vegetables, more leaves, the rest of the hot stones, a sprinkle of water, and the hole was hastily covered with earth. Three hours later, a delicious meal would be taken out of this virtual pressure cooker!

But we didn't wait as long as that. After chatting further with the leaders, trying to find out more about their ideas and customs, we returned home. We had had about enough of the noise, sorrow and evil.

The next afternoon, a Government officer arrived from Koroba. After talking with those involved, and seeing the body, he confronted the accused, who confessed to the crime and was led off to Koroba. At a Supreme Court trial, he received the death sentence, later repealed to five years' imprisonment.

He spent the time in the capital, Port Moresby, where he learned all sorts of things – truck driving, brick-making, reading and religious instruction. When he returned home he found that he had grown completely away from his people and only stayed in the valley a couple of weeks. We did not hear of him again.

But what had begun all this? In the Yuna culture, we learned, single men regard women as completely taboo. When this girl (who had been married but had left her husband) approached this young man, he was so frightened that he killed her.

A Handmade Airstrip

Quite a good start had been made on the airstrip by now, but for a couple of weeks after the murder the whole valley seethed with unrest and only a handful of men came to work.

What a task it was!

It took thirteen months to the first landing and then there was still more to be done after that. Work went on five days most weeks, with as many as four hundred men on the job. First, all the black soil had to be removed and heaped out of the way. Ivor criss-crossed high places with drains, cut down to the correct level and grade. In areas where the level had to be built up, sticks were put in to the right height for filling. The slope was maximum and it had to be cambered so that the centre was higher than the sides to ensure proper drainage during rainstorms.

Each clan worked the section that was assigned to them. Many of these men were bitter enemies, never having worked together, rarely having met except on the battlefield. Many had old scores to settle. It took the eye of a hawk to foresee trouble brewing and to stop it before it got serious. There were a number of incidents that were both humorous and nasty.

One day, Ivor noticed work stop in a certain section and heard a heated argument going on. A young fellow reckoned that an old man owed him a pig. He claimed that the compensation the old man had paid when he killed his grandfather had been inadequate. The incident had taken place many years before and he had only heard of it second hand, but he was aspiring to be a leader and this was an opportunity to show his strength.

When Ivor arrived he was standing over the old chap with his shining new steel axe. No one had done anything to interfere – rather they were enjoying the drama of it all. With the co-operation of some of the leaders, Ivor got him tied up with vines until he cooled down a bit. Then he sat down and had a long quiet chat with him. The young fellow responded well. He did become an acknowledged leader. He confessed Christ as Saviour and was baptised. For a while he ran well, but has since stumbled.

Another day we were sitting having lunch when we noticed one whole section of men walk off the job and come up the track to the house. They were seething with rage. "That group working near us, they started an argument," they declared self-righteously. "We are not going to work by them anymore. They can have it to themselves."

The leaders went back down with Ivor and after about an hour's quiet reasoning the whole thing was settled peaceably. How relieved the complainers were. They had only walked out because they were getting the worst of it. Everyone else looked on astonished. Two groups of fellows settling an argument peaceably? An unheard-of way of doing things!

Mostly the leaders co-operated to the limit of their knowledge as to how to go about work, but at times they contradicted Ivor's instructions when he turned his back, and whole sections of work had to be re-done. Perhaps they felt that they were losing prestige by obeying someone else.

As he worked with them Ivor came to love and respect these men. They were men of iron character, hard to handle at this stage perhaps, but what potential for the days ahead when the Lord would do the wonders He had promised. He soon learned, if he had not fully realised it before, that he had to be firm and tough too, if he was to command respect and truly represent the Lord he served.

I once heard a missionary in another part of the Highlands say, "As a new missionary I didn't like to take a tough line with these men. I felt we should show love by being kind and gentle. But after a while I came to realise that they regarded me as a weak man, and not only me but the God about whom I taught. I was His only representative to them, and what they saw in me was what they thought He was like. It was a sobering thought. When they failed to respect me, I realised that they were thinking that God was as weak as I was appearing to be, and that they would not respect Him either."

It was always a thrill when an MAF pilot came to have a look at us and buzz the workmen. Ivor was up in the plane on one occasion. They were heading for Koroba and he asked Harold if they could take a look at the Pori airstrip first. Harold changed course minutely, calculating it dead on. They crossed the last mountains and there was Pori right below. Being fully loaded, they did not descend into the valley but circled above and got a clear look. They laughed from their bird's-eye view as they saw men excitedly drop tools and rush wildly in every direction, not knowing which way to run.

When a pilot came in low the workmen would dive into the ditches or over the side, screaming with a mixture of fear and excitement. If we knew ahead that the plane was coming, we would send word out in order to get a big gang in and give them something to arouse their enthusiasm for the job.

We had several air drops of supplies during the time the airstrip was under construction. The first was arranged for two days after Ivor came over with intention to settle. He arranged it thus in order to have time to clear the drop site of anything that might damage the cargo. Strip-work was not as yet under way in earnest. Ivor arrived late afternoon one day and was just about to pay the carriers the next morning when the shout went up that a plane was coming.

Clearing ground for the airstrip.

Getting the levels right.

"Oh, it must be a Government one, just going past," he replied.

"But it's a yellow one, and it's coming down here!" they yelled back.

With that Ivor went to see. It was an MAF plane all right—just circling to have a look, he thought. But then the plane turned and he could see that the door was off. It was here to do the drop! He hadn't even been down to look at the drop site.

Too late now. Everyone rushed down the track arriving just as the plane came in for a final check. There was Kay standing over the cargo in the back with a rope tied around his waist, his hair streaming wildly above him. Ivor glanced down the drop site. Sticks, stones and stumps of sharp bamboo were everywhere. He cried to God that the load might not be ruined. Then the plane was back again. Lower, lower, he could see Kay very clearly now working frantically to get as much as possible through the doorway before Harold shouted, "Stop." Round again and he got it all out.

There were bags of salt packed inside a second large loose sack, and drums of nails, which sounded like machine guns going off as they rolled and bounced. Harold had skilfully manoeuvred the plane and directed Kay so that the goods landed at the top of the incline and rolled, to minimise the impact. Nothing hit the stumps or jagged limestone rocks. Everything was recovered in good condition. One of the bags of salt had not even burst the inner plastic.

Harold told us afterwards that he was sorry that he had to change the date, but he couldn't fit it in later in the week.

The drop that was the greatest thrill of all was the one he made for us on Christmas Eve. Two single men had walked over the mountains to spend the holiday week with us and we were looking forward to serving them some Christmas lamb, but it hadn't arrived. Then in the afternoon, about one o'clock, came the sound we were waiting for, a Cessna 180 aircraft. There at

Boulders on the airstrip!

Moving boulders the Yuna way.

the controls was Harold, with Neville, Ivor's brother, in the back looking most uncomfortable. Ivor was busily occupied with Harold's movie-camera which he had sent to us beforehand to get a photographic record of the operation. Hundreds of men were standing by and many women were peeping out from further away under the trees or up by the house. A strong wind tossed the little plane about, but I knew it had to come in lower yet. Ivor struggled to do the right things with the camera.

One, two, three circuits, and Neville had everything out. Bag after bag of mail, obviously stuffed with parcels from loving families and friends at home. The bright red bag with the frozen meat in it was there in the air too, along with bags of salt and other goods. The salt was a Christmas present for the men who had worked so hard. Then, with a final swoop over and a cheery wave, they were gone. Once again there was a full recovery of goods.

'Moon' after 'moon' the work continued. Many thousands of cubic metres of earth were shovelled into bags and carried away. Two long poles passed longwise through either side inside the bags and out through the bottom corners made a stretcher that could be carried by two men with less than one tenth of a metre of clay at a time. It was tedious work. Then they came on to great outcrops of limestone. They chipped away at them with sledge-hammers, carrying away what they could. Great fires were built in a trench around the rocks. When they grew hot, a bucket of water, well aimed, would cause an explosion and remove a large lump; then the fires were stoked up again and the process repeated. Some lumps took weeks to be cut down to a size small enough for them to be dug out and rolled away.

All the fillings had to be rammed. As some dumped bags of earth, other men were there with big wooden posts to ram the clay hard. Once, in an area where they had dodged the labour of ramming it properly, a tremendous slip occurred, taking with it a small portion of the runway. It was quite a shock to them all –

and a lesson to those who thought that they knew a better way of doing the job than the way they had been told to follow.

Finally, opening day arrived. The date for the initial landing on the strip had been carefully planned with MAF, but Max Flavel called up in the morning to say that he had still not received permission from the Department of Civil Aviation in Port Moresby for the landing. However, he would come in anyway with a load for Koroba. The telegram could be relayed to him in the air if it was sent in time.

Mid-morning, when he passed over en route to Koroba, we explained to the crowd of two thousand that he had to go to Koroba first and unload, then come back with an empty plane so that he could test the strip. They waited noisily, anxiously, as the rainclouds gathered nearer and nearer. Later we were relieved to see the sky clear again.

Max unloaded at Koroba with still no telegram, and, good-naturedly, he waited on. He knew that it would be beyond the Pori folk to understand about things like the long delays that red tape often involves. He didn't want to disappoint them, but finally he had to call up to say that he must return to Wewak. He came overhead and a mighty roar went up from the excited crowd. Then as he circled again but did not land, Ivor tried to explain that he was not allowed to do so without the permit. Away went the plane and we wondered for a minute or two just what the crowd would do, but Ivor continued to try to get them to understand, and to assure them that he would certainly be back in a few days when the telegram was eventually sent.

We were just heading back to the house when a mighty shout went up. "He's coming back!"

"No," we said, "it must be another plane." We didn't dare let them raise their hopes again. But it was our plane coming back. Five minutes out from us, the telegram had been sent, so Max turned back.

There was a hush as everyone held their breath while he did a final circuit.

This was the moment.

After all those months of work it was a tremendous excitement for them. How could I describe our own feelings? Having been completely cut off from the outside world for so long, it was exciting to feel that we belonged to it again. Occasionally, I had dreamt of carrying Ivor out over the mountains with a broken leg or appendicitis! It had never really worried me, for we were in the Lord's hands, but it was a nice feeling, nevertheless, to know that those days were soon to be behind us.

Lower…lower…the little yellow Cessna was approaching the low end of the strip; now…down…down…it seemed so far down, watching from the top end of the strip. Then his wheels were down, just over twenty metres up the strip, the engine roared as he came over the brow of the hill and pulled up a few yards from where we were standing. A thousand screaming men and boys mobbed the plane, forgetting Ivor's careful instructions completely in their excitement.

Then the headmen remembered and began hitting the boys and ordering the fellows back – as though anyone would take notice! Finally, we elbowed our way in and got the door open enough for Max to get out. A young new pilot was on board with Max. He was obviously wondering what he had struck.

They spent some time inspecting the strip while the Yuna men inspected the plane. The women too were edging in along the banks to get a closer look.

By now it was well after mid-day. The weather was closing in over the central ranges and they had to get along. After a lot of shouting the people were hustled away from the plane. Then the engine roared and they were off down the slope. For a moment the plane was out of our sight, then up it came climbing easily to soar off to the north.

The pilot's view for the first landing.

Taxying uphill on the first landing.

So disappointment turned to tremendous joy.

All this time nothing had been paid for the work being done; at their request it was held over until the job was finished. For months we had been collecting mother-of-pearl shells, axes, spades, knives, bush-knives (up to 30 cms long) as well as the usual small goods: matches, razor-blades and mirrors, besides the ever-popular salt.

Ivor had endeavoured to keep a roll-book for the work done, but in the beginning many of the men were too frightened to tell him their names or let him write them down. They believed that for us to have their names meant that we could work black magic over them and cause illness or death. This was one of the reasons why so many dodged the patrols when the Government made the census in the early days – thus population figures could double after a year or two. After a while they realised that there was nothing to fear, and we kept fairly complete records for the second half of the job.

What a headache it was to work out what was due to each man. And when the figure was worked out, it then had to be related to goods. This took a number of late nights. The headmen co-operated well and we were able to find out who had worked all the time, just now and then, or half the time.

It was arranged to take two days to give out the goods. The first date was set for Saturday, 26th June. Ivor's brother Neville was there at the time and his help was very much appreciated.

Early in the morning hundreds of fellows were around, either down on the strip or waiting expectantly outside the house. Everyone had come to see what went on, even if it was not his day to be paid. This was their big day.

Several groups had said, "We are waiting to see what your pay is like." What they meant was, "If you prove to be fair and honest then we will accept you completely, and will come and listen well to what you are teaching."

All were more than satisfied. There were one or two mistakes, but these were sorted out happily and all went away delighted. After a 3 p.m. lunch, we worked on for several more hours, preparing for the further payments to be made on Monday.

At six on Monday morning, shouts were heard all over the valley, and by seven, hundreds of men had assembled. We filled two large tin trunks with goods and set off for the strip with a list of three hundred names. The men sat down in line in their clan groups. One group at a time, the men were called up to the table where Ivor sat with their leader standing beside him. A few adjustments were made regarding valid complaints. Some other complaints, not so valid, were settled once they could understand that pay was given only in proportion to the work they had done. At first some who had not worked much could not understand why they should get less than others who had worked more. Finally, all went away satisfied, in fact most jubilant.

How hard it was for stone-age men to understand such matters. So elementary for us, they were thoroughly puzzling to them. Not that the men were less intelligent – far from it, but they lacked experience. Our four-year-old was daily learning things that were foreign concepts to grown men living around him.

We were so grateful to the Lord that all went well. There was no incident of consequence – certainly no fighting which could so easily have occurred with quick-tempered, uncontrollable men who had so recently been deadly enemies.

Now MAF gave us a weekly service – bread, mail, freezer goods, groceries. The Department of Civil Aviation thought that our local name of Ayuguali was too much of a tongue-twister, so we chose Pori, the name of the river running down the valley.

Everyone wants to see the plane

Play Day

In Papua New Guinea, as Government influence was spreading, one of the things the Government tried to do was to give the people new social outlets. As they stopped harmful practices like fighting, they tried to give them something better to do. One institution that became a national one was a play-day at Christmas-time. With sports, an archery competition and a tug-of-war, it was a day looked forward to by everyone. There were prizes and food and then dancing to follow. As each new area was opened up, the Christmas play-day became the thing to do. Gradually, the Government withdrew financial support, but continued to organise the event. Everyone dressed up in their best headgear and finery according to the local customs. In the main, the missions had done the same thing.

After the airstrip was completed and life had begun to settle down to normal again, we decided we would have a play-day. It was mid-June and the first time most of our folk had had anything to do with organised games. We got the workmen practising beforehand. I can still feel my sides aching as I look back on them rolling helplessly around the back yard, trying three-legged racing. They just couldn't get the idea of keeping in step and in time. They tried sack-racing and their enthusiasm was once again their undoing, and they all ended up in a large inverted heap screaming with laughter.

The morning of the great day finally arrived and hundreds of people were milling around, not knowing what to expect or do.

A feast was prepared and put into the ovens. Then, somehow, we got order and started trying to organise them.

First the flat races in age groups. I had the hilarious task of holding the rope. No one could be persuaded to run into it. They had to jump it. Prizes: a box of matches for the first, and a razor blade for the second. They were thrilled to get them. The last race was for the recognised leaders. They asked Ivor to run with them, and left him standing.

A crossbar was set over a pit of broken-up ground for pillow fighting with a rice sack stuffed with dry grass, while for the high jump there was a bamboo pole. It was completely beyond them to work in teams. What matter – they just took turns and had a wonderful time.

Last and best of all was the greasy pole. A long straight pole, seven and a half metres long, was brought in from the bush and stripped of bark and any knobs or notches that could give a toe-hold. Then it was thoroughly rubbed over with waste oil and erected vertically in a clear space. A cross bar on top held the prizes. Highest and farthest was a large shining pearl shell, then an axe, a large mirror, a bush knife and a tomahawk.

The word was given and they all tried to start up at once, boys, young men, and even some older men. Each had a piece of old rag trying to wipe off the oil and get a grip with hands and ankles held in a circlet of vine. Finally, a line of several were on their way up. Then the top one slipped down on to the shoulders of the one beneath him and the whole line slid to the ground. How the crowd roared! Mbaluba the headman rushed in to put more oil on the pole.

It was two hours later, when we were sitting up on a little knoll of grass watching while we sipped a cup of tea, that a roar of victory went up. The first man grabbed the pearl shell and hugged it to him. Then he obligingly handed the second man's choice to him and the third and so on, until the prizes were gone and they slid down, exhausted heroes. They were unrecognisable beneath the black tenacious oil. Someone handed them a gourd of water.

And now the feast was ready. Steaming legs of pork were handed out with the vegetable of choice and a noisy silence reigned for half-an-hour. Then filled, tired and ever so happy they set off for home.

Carrying in the tree pole

Christmas Day games

One Day at a Time

How I wish you could have experienced a day at Pori to see how we lived in those early days. The birds were singing, so it was round about six a.m. Here just a few degrees south of the equator dawn came suddenly and at the same time all the year round. It varied only about fifteen minutes, and the birds were our alarm. Ivor moved outside to call, "Hanabe...oh". A bleary-eyed fifteen-year-old emerged from the smoke-blackened hut nearby and came inside to light the fire in the wood stove. A whistle-blast aroused the workmen sleeping in their house just over the hill-side.

Meanwhile I slipped out and made a cup of coffee from the thermos flask. We returned to read and pray. Then, at 6.45, Ivor turned on the radio receiver for the inter-mission station sched. He set the transmitter to stand by, in case someone should call.

I listened in while preparing porridge and fried bananas.

"Delta Oscar, Delta Papa," Neville's voice came in clearly from Koroba, where he and Joyce were relieving Kay and Gwen Liddle for furlough.

"Delta Papa from Delta Oscar, receiving you loud and clear. Go ahead, over," Ivor replied.

"Good morning Ivor. Your carriers have just left with mail, a drum of flour, a carton of matches, and a 200-litre drum."

"Roger, roger, Nev...Many thanks." Ivor concluded the conversation. The empty fuel drum was one we had bought from MAF for setting the copper in to boil the clothes.

Someone else called in. It was Cecil Parish from Yellow River. "It has been raining all night. The strip will be closed until midday. I will call again with a further report," he said to Frank Bielby.

"Roger, Ces. I'll let MAF know," he replied.

There was silence for a few minutes; then the programme manager from MAF Wewak called in.

"This is VL9, India Quebec, Wewak, calling all stations. Good morning. The programme for today is as follows: Bravo Victor Kilo will be going, Wirui, (the base at Wewak), Green River, Amanab, Lumi, Nuku, Wirui." (etc., etc.). He listed the day's work for each plane. Then, "Any station with traffic—will you call please?"

A Baptist missionary called to ask for some priority items of loading for the next flight. A Church of Christ missionary called in to say that they had a new airstrip ready to be opened and were wondering about fixing a date for this. An Assemblies of God missionary called to say that they had a seriously ill patient needing transport to a hospital as soon as possible. The programme for one of the planes was altered accordingly. Frank Bielby passed on the message from Yellow River and so on and so on. What would we have done without MAF? We just couldn't have existed in those outback spots without their economical, efficient service.

At ten past seven we sat down to breakfast. By half past the workmen had eaten and were waiting outside for roll call. All were present. Good. One was asked to recite the Ten Commandments. Another enumerated the seven days of Creation. (Could you have done so? I'd have had to have thought hard too.) Then Ivor went over the story of Bartimaeus, the lesson for the week. Two of the fellows prayed and then they were briefed for the day's work.

"Four of you carry water, please. What is that? The spring is drying up? Well, you will have to go to the far away one. Try not to disturb the mud, won't you?" This particular water hole was hard to get at and it was hard to keep the water clean. "One of you go and dig the potatoes down by the chapel site, please. When those of you who are carrying water have filled the drum you can cut firewood. Here, take this piece for a mark, please. You won't cut it any longer than that, will you? Later you can all go down and finish the thatching on your new house."

They slipped past the window, calling out for women to bring thatching grass and sweet potatoes.

We paused a few minutes for prayer together, then Ivor set off to visit a sick woman. It would take an hour-and-a-half to reach her, but at this stage they would have been afraid to carry a woman in to us. Nor could she have been persuaded to leave her home ground, for if she were to die away from it, they believed her spirit would be in enemy territory. So, at these early stages in the work, we went to them. She may have died soon afterwards, for she had a fast-growing cancer of the breast. It was a raw, infected mess, but injections of penicillin were able to bring her fever down as it arrested the infection, and this made her feel a lot more comfortable.

Ivor was seeking to teach her of the Saviour. The last time we visited her she said, "I'm listening to your words. I want God's fashion." Just as he was about to go, someone called out, "Misini" (missionary), "A hawk is circling the hen run." I waited quietly... bang. Yodels went up, and excited boys rushed to get the feathers and a mouthful of protein each. Now, what was I doing? Oh, yes, setting yeast to make bread and "Hanabe, the fire is almost out," I called to the houseboy.

"Hagini, hagini," a persistent voice at the door called me. "Come and buy our sweet potatoes." I placed a spoonful of salt on to the leaf they each held and their faces beamed with delight. A mother dropped a little on to the ground so her toddler got down and licked it up. They had never had real salt before.

Now I needed to get back to knead the bread. Whoops, I had to wait a minute. Hanabe was struggling in through the door with two full buckets of water. Two of the workmen passed by the window. A long pole stretching between their shoulders held two swinging buckets of water. It was not slopping much, as they had bunches of bracken fern on top of the water.

Good, that was the bread set to rise. Now what? Before I could decide another called, "Misisi, Misisi." (Mrs. – a European woman)

"What is it?" I asked.

"I have cut my toe with a spade." It was one of the men off the airstrip job.

"Sorry, my brother," I replied in good idiom. "Go and wash your foot and I will bandage it for you."

A few moments later he returned, his foot dripping a mixture of mud and blood. It was quite a deep gash across the nail bed of his big toe. I had a lot of those sorts of injuries to deal with until they learned to handle steel axes and sharp shovels.

Back to the housework...or was I? "Misisi," Hanabe called from where he was grinding dried corn for the hens. "Some boys have brought bananas for you to buy."

"I want matches," one said.

"I'll have money," said the other.

Back to light the kerosine iron. I stopped and listened for a moment – the familiar drone of an aeroplane was growing louder...where was it? Up there in the north...yes, it was a yellow one, so it must have been an MAF pilot. He was descending...he was coming in to buzz the strip...back and forth, back and forth, he gave the fellows a tremendous thrill, then came up and buzzed the house too. I waved from the front lawn and was cheered to see Doug Hunt's smiling face clearly as he passed.

Now I needed to get back to that iron. This time I got it going and turned on a tape-recording of Yuna language drills to listen to as I worked. An hour later, with only a few garments to do, there came another interruption.

"Come and buy the thatching grass," one of the workmen

called. "There are a lot of women here waiting and we are ready to put it on the house now."

I took the old saucepan of salt down to where they were lined up beside their bundles, each holding a wide leaf ready for the salt. Most of them came on up to the house to listen to last Sunday's sermon, recorded for them on the tape recorder.

As I returned to the ironing I glanced outside and saw a shirt down on the airstrip. Ivor must have arrived back. Why, it couldn't have been a quarter-to-twelve yet. Oh well, the rest of the ironing had to wait. What should we have for lunch? There were lots of tomatoes, and a tinned sausage would be tasty with them.

Ivor came in just as I finished setting the table and blew the whistle for the workmen to stop for a cold, baked sweet potato. It was a relief to him to take off his wet muddy boots and drink a large glass of water.

"The Lord is working in the sick woman's heart," he told me after a few mouthfuls of food. "They asked that you and I would pray for them every day."

After lunch he went down to supervise the work on the airstrip and have a meeting with the men before they went home. I enjoyed a siesta reading from one of Isobel Kuhn's challenging, inspiring books. Then the afternoon flew by with language study, the writing of an article for the NZBTI Writer's Course and some mending and gardening. I put in a few lettuce and carrot seeds and collected silver beet and swede for dinner. Here, where there were no seasons, we planted about once a month enough to last us for a month.

At about four o'clock, a group of women came in on their way home from the day's gardening. One had some sweet potatoes to sell and another had a sick baby. She was very frightened and I lingered to chat with her after praying for the child and giving it penicillin for pneumonia. Now it was half-past-four – time for the knock-off whistle.

The workmen, who were also the week-end preachers fanning out all over the valley, came for another class on the story of Bartimaeus. "Lord, apply it to their hearts," I prayed as I listened to Ivor as he drilled them on the facts and then explained the application. Only then would they be able to give a message for their people and not just a story.

At five Ivor settled in his office to prepare for the evening meeting. At two minutes past five there was an urgent call. Someone called out excitedly, "Two of the workers are having a big argument! Please, come quickly."

One of the younger fellows, about fifteen, had been playing when he should have been working. One of the older ones, about eighteen, had taken discipline into his own hands with a heavy stick. After a long argument the younger one was almost insane with rage. "I'll chop him with my axe!" he was shouting, over and over again. It took some firm talking to calm him down, and this also provided another opportunity to teach that it is possible to settle differences peaceably if God is in control.

Half-past five was sched. time again, and we listened as missionaries conversed. There was medical traffic first. One of the sisters from Green River discussed the condition of a sick baby with Doctor John Sturt and a mother came up to ask for advice about her child with an eye infection. Then Don McGregor called to let Gerald Wunsch know that there was sufficient loading at Lumi for five carriers. Gerry and Betty were living at Inebu at the time, a full day's walk away.

"Right," said Gerry. "I'll get them away in the morning. They will be there to sleep tomorrow night and leave early next morning."

Later, with dinner over, we enjoyed a quiet stroll outside. The wind had dropped and everything was sparkling clean after a heavy shower. With the sun sinking behind the mountains the whole valley was topped with pink cloud.

What was that sound?...I listened...yes, there it was again. Yodelling was coming from up the valley, the tired but jubilant voices of carriers nearing home. They had been on the track from Koroba for twelve hours. We stood and watched them as they came down the hillside, dirty, weary, hungry, thirsty, but so glad to see us, happy to be helping us to stay on with them. One poor fellow appeared very worried.

"I fell over," he told me. "Are the eggs all broken?"

I opened them up and found a couple cracked but nothing wasted, and he smiled, relieved.

"Go now," Ivor said. "Eat and sleep well. Come in the morning for your pay."

Before we had everything unpacked the men arrived for Bible Class. Thirty of them crowded onto our kitchen floor and really enjoyed their study. Would they give their hearts and lives to Him soon? How we coveted them for Him, to become spiritual men with a ministry to their own people. I prayed quietly for them as I sat on the other side of the door sewing.

As they left we sipped a cup of Milo together and read the letters from home. I glanced out the window and there were their flares shining in the darkness as they wound along the track. They carried a resinous type of pine and lit it as they left.

How wonderful it was to get a letter from my mother every week and several others from relatives and friends. So the day ended with a note of praise and thanks. It was a privilege to be called to serve Him and so very wonderful to be used of Him.

Our evening thought was:

I no longer live, but Christ lives in me. The life I now live in the body, I live by faith in the Son of God, who loved me, and gave himself for me.

Galatians 2:20

Local Preachers

Immediately after Ivor set up camp at Pori he began collecting a group of promising young men around him. Initially they came to help with odd jobs, but as they proved themselves to be good workers they were employed more permanently. They would work for a few months, then go home for a few weeks to make gardens. Thus they never became dependent on us for their support.

As they worked, they watched our lives, and talked with us continually as practical lessons were applied from incidents that arose. Besides the regular meetings, Bible lessons were given twice a day, which they were expected to attend and rarely missed.

Their tasks included carrying water daily to fill the 200-litre drum which was our only storage, chopping wood for the fuel stove, preparing timber straight from the bush for buildings and plaiting flattened-out bamboo matting. How their faces puckered in concentration as they tried to trim battens. The final product that they were so proud of was more like a corkscrew than a support for the brown paper ceiling, but in time they became more proficient, some even going on to work with Dick Hedley, the carpenter who came from New Zealand to build for us. It was great to see what Dick was able to get them to do, though they were illiterate, and he was only able to converse with them by a word here and there.

Before long they got tired of walking to and fro each day. We also found it unsatisfactory. On a wet dull morning they would be an hour or more late. On similar afternoons they wanted to leave long before knock-off time. One day it became very dull about half-past-three, and some agitator started the rumour that it was later and that we were not letting on, in order to get more work out of them. Eventually someone came out with what all the grumbling was about and Ivor explained. They were not convinced, but later when the day drew on into a fine evening they realised how silly it had all been and had a good laugh about it the next morning. The Yuna had a great sense of humour. They loved a joke, would take one against themselves and turn round and pull your leg a mile too!

However, they wanted a house on the station to save all the travelling, and we agreed. Used as they were to sleeping in tiny low houses and keeping warm by the fire, we wondered how best to accommodate a bigger group. Certainly, we wanted the place big enough to stand up in, with a door and plenty of window light somewhere too. Finally, we settled on a blanket each (not to be taken home), and a two-roomed place with bunks at one end and a fire for cooking at the other.

A site was chosen on the lee of a small knoll. No-one mentioned that it was a spirit grove, but after the house was finished they were all too frightened to sleep in it. Using this as another spiritual opportunity, Ivor challenged them to pray and to trust God to protect them. Finally, a group of them bravely decided to sleep one night. Whether they slept or not we wondered, but they spent the night in the house and the rest joined them, trembling but triumphant.

One by one they fell sick, some seriously with cerebral malaria and pneumonia, as well as less serious complaints. "You see," everyone said, "You have forsaken the spirit fashion. Then you go and build a house in their domain and of course you get sick. Quickly now, sacrifice to the spirits before you all die!"

Fearfully, they wavered and looked to us for reassurance. We prayed for them, and with them, and gave appropriate drugs as we had them. Two nearly died.

"This is a real burden," Ivor commented at the time. "So much depends on what happens to our closest followers at this stage. If they die it will be attributed to their forsaking spirit worship. This is Satan's bondage, and they are fighting to be freed from it and to set an example to others to do the same. The majority around are still firmly in his clutches. If they recover, many will be encouraged to make the break and cease to worship evil spirits and kill pigs to them in times of sickness. We are trusting the Lord to bless the medicines being given and to heal completely."

All made a full recovery without any return to the appeasement of evil spirits.

We prayed much about the selection of these fellows. Many came seeking permanent work, but we were not just looking for workmen. In a very real sense they were to be disciples who would learn and then in turn go out and teach others. Only through such helpers could we hope to cover the population of the area with regular teaching. We had some from nearby, but it was from the areas further out that we were most anxious to get keen alert young men.

As we prayed, the Lord sent them in. After we got to know the area better, we found that He had sent representatives from every clan in our 'parish'. Truly it was the Lord's work! As we served Him, He frequently did more through us than we were aware of.

They were a great mixture of personalities, causing us many a laugh and many a headache – or should I say heartache? But on the whole, they responded to the Lord and went on well with Him. There was one we called 'the clown'. He could mime and create good humour in almost any situation. He was always playing tricks on us and on the others. How they loved to tease

– us as well as themselves. They could pull our leg with a straight face and then go off roaring with laughter to tell the story.

One young fellow just couldn't stop talking. One day I got tired of the sound of his voice as they worked planting grass runners around the house. I said, "Oh, Pore, you're a gasbag."

"What is that?" he asked, so I explained. He was delighted, and coined the word 'gatabaga' and was known by it for some time thereafter.

One promising lad was drowned one day when out on the lake with a flimsy raft – these people do not swim. Neville appeared on the scene just a minute or two after he disappeared, but failed to trace him in the muddy water.

One or two left us to go to the coast on a two-year working contract.

As the message began to take root, it was fascinating to stand by and watch the Holy Spirit at work. Some just gradually blossomed out. Like a flower bud opening to the sun, so they responded to His love. Others came under deep conviction and resisted. There were dark days as we tried to tolerate and love them through those rebellious stages. How wonderfully worthwhile it was to see them radiantly transformed as they finally did yield control to the Saviour.

So, week after week they worked and learned. Often they went on long walks with Ivor and, chatting in a relaxed atmosphere, tongues were loosened, and hearts opened up. Problems were brought to light and discussed fully with appropriate Scriptures. In this way Ivor learned a lot about their beliefs and customs, especially if an older man was with the party.

After several months, the Lord thrust the first of them out on their own to preach for the first time. He laid Ivor aside with 'flu. He had planned to go out preaching the next day and word had already gone out telling them when to gather, so he called in Pita and Tiaga and challenged them to go and give these people God's talk. Their response was enthusiastic, but they were nervous about it too, so Ivor ran through the stories of the Creation and Fall with them.

The next morning they came in for a time of prayer before leaving. As we watched them go, we were aware of the possibilities of development under God's hand – just two young fellows starting out to preach. The prayer burden for them was with us all day. Then, late in the afternoon, they returned.

One had walked six hours and had had a meeting with about a hundred and forty people. The other walked four hours and had had two meetings, one of a hundred and twenty, and the second of a hundred and fifty or so. They reported attentive hearings and firm invitations to return again soon. Pita reported that he was told of a sick man so went off the track quite a way to visit him. He said, "I think he will die soon. I gave him God's talk so that he can be ready to go to Heaven."

Needless to say their hearts were glowing. We had prayer and a cup of tea together before they left wearily for their evening meal of sweet potatoes.

From this start it was not long before they were fanning out all over the valley each Saturday to preach in their own areas. Mostly they went in twos. One would lead the singing of the two choruses that they had at the time, the reciting of the Ten Commandments, a few memory verses, and a prayer; then the second one would pass on the story they had been learning all the week. When one of them forgot a point the other one would prompt him, so they quickly became used to standing in front of a crowd and expressing themselves fluently and positively. At first, their preaching was little more than the passing on of the bones of a Bible story, but later as they began to grow spiritually themselves, so they had an application to add from their own experience.

Sowing the Word

Some asked, "What do you teach such people? Where do you start? How do you go about it?"

Here is an outline of one way that it was done – the way that God used so mightily here. It was not possible to preach Christ's crucifixion to those who had never heard of Him, nor so much as heard that there was a God. There had to be months of building up background knowledge first. An occasional person would be born again after hearing very little, but those were the exceptions, not the rule.

First, we taught the fact of God. This one theme went on daily for two months based on the creation story. God is spirit, good, all-powerful, always present, righteous, holy, faithful, loving. Then the fact of sin through the story of the Fall. From the story of Cain and Abel we taught the fruits of the root of sin—Anger, Murder, Deceit, and later Righteousness by Faith by way of sacrifice. Judgement was taught through the story of the Flood, then God's standard by teaching the Ten Commandments.

And after all that—perhaps a year's teaching—it was possible to teach the Birth of Jesus, some stories of His life, and then on to the Trial, Crucifixion and Resurrection.

Imagine how difficult it was telling the Crucifixion story to someone who had never heard it before! Then the Resurrection…

After weeks and weeks spent on these things they were thrilled to learn about Pentecost and the Person of the Holy Spirit. Now it was time to point out that they must personally take Christ as their Saviour. Perhaps the story of the Great White Throne would be the one the Lord would take up and with which He would challenge them at that stage.

The teaching of illiterate men, completely ignorant about the Bible story, however intelligent they were, was a long, slow process. It had to be precept upon precept – each repeated dozens of times over.

We spent eighteen months covering all this ground, and it was at this stage that the reaping commenced. Some experienced missionaries said it happened too soon. We were cautious – almost frightened – when dozens started declaring that Jesus was their Saviour. What Spirit was this of? Was it really of God? It certainly was – all of Him – and nothing could stop what He was doing at that time. But I am getting ahead of my story.

Early Reactions

The people's reactions as they heard the various stories for the first time were interesting, amusing, even thrilling. We found it was very wonderful that they would ask and answer questions freely, and discuss a point back and forth. This enabled us to know just how they were reacting, how much they were grasping and which way their thoughts were going. We learned a lot about what they had formerly believed and how they had lived.

When we were teaching the creation story it came out that each clan group had a different legend concerning their origin. One group said that their first father was the son of a huge snake. This creature was still living in a patch of bush just across the river. No one could see it and continue to live. Nothing would have enticed one of them to go in there. Another group said that their forefather was the son of the headman of the evil spirits. He had five sons and they were the forbears of their five sub-clans.

After hearing a message on the Fall, one man said, "We are like our ancestors that the Bible tells us about. We are held by Satan, but now we want God's way. We will come and hear you give us God's talk."

One day on trek, Ivor killed a snake. A boy who had just been listening to the story of the Garden of Eden said, "Kill it well. It is Satan."

The Ten Commandments were being discussed. "You must give us this talk often," someone said. "Then the people can learn

God's laws and stop following Satan's way."

One young leader, spirited and loud, had been adamant that he had never done anything wrong, until one day, after only a few months' teaching, he said, "We are like Adam and Eve who left God's good way and took hold of Satan's bad way. We, their descendants, have followed our forefathers and have this bad way of life too. We too do all sorts of bad things. We can't help doing them. We are just as bad." So a consciousness of sin was developing, even if he was still excusing himself from personal responsibility for it.

One Sunday morning, we were disappointed when only a handful of people turned up for the service, but as there was only a small group of keen ones present, they started talking and asking questions freely. The prepared sermon was put aside as a question-and-answer session developed.

"Did Satan come to earth first, or Jesus?"

"Well, is Jesus going to ever come again?"

One old man pointed to the group of small boys sitting together up the front. "Will Jesus take these small boys up to Heaven after He comes back again? We old people will perhaps be dead by then. So will we have to go to the place of fire?" And it was only a few months since they had first heard the name of God. Truly they were a prepared people.

What opportunities we had. You could never feel, as some people thought, that your life was being thrown away, when those Yuna – of great value in God's sight – were being won to Him.

On several occasions men came asking Ivor to pray that they might be enabled to find a lost pig. Formerly they would have sacrificed to the spirits and sought their help. Now they wanted to turn to God and leave the spirits, but they didn't quite know how. Their faith in the spirits was being shattered, and it seemed that this God that the missionary prayed to did have power to help. Some genuinely wanted to prove Him. Sensing the mixed motives, Ivor would challenge them, "Truly God can see everything. He knows where the pig is. But He also knows your thoughts. Do you really intend to follow God's way or are you just making a convenience of Him? He won't have you do that." Then he would pray. Several of them came back, jubilant because they had gone right to where the pig was. One man found his sow with a litter of young ones. He said, "Truly God sees everything. My heart is happy towards Him." So by these simple means, God truly drew men towards himself.

The weather-pattern had changed and the afternoon rain was coming as early as midday every day. It not only stopped the work on the airstrip, but also meant that the men rushed off without having a meeting. At devotions one morning we prayed specifically that the Lord would enable a meeting to be held that day. About midday, with a big gang working well, the rain clouds started to gather. The leaders came to Ivor, "You tell us that God answers prayer. You tell us that God made and controls everything. Well, look at all these men looking at all those clouds. They are going to run off any time now. Ask God to turn the rain away."

So just there, in the middle of a crowd of unsaved men, Ivor prayed out loud, asking simply that it would not rain. And the Lord further showed Himself to them as the clouds moved away. The men worked a full day and heard another story from His word before going home.

Then came the first time ever that they heard the crucifixion story. One leader got up and said, "You have been teaching us about this God. We have believed you and started to lose our fears of Satan. Some of us have ceased to worship him. Now, you tell us Jesus is dead!" He stalked off down the airstrip, angry, disappointed and frightened.

"Just a minute Ndago," Ivor called after him. "Truly Jesus died, but – listen: on the third day he rose again. He is not only alive, Ndago, but alive again after having once been dead. He conquered death as well as Satan!"

Hibuya was deep in thought for a few minutes and then said, "What was God doing while those bad men were killing His Son? Was He just looking on, doing nothing?" It was quite obvious what he would have done to anyone who dared touch his son.

Preaching one day on the love of God, Ivor said, "Jesus died for us because He loves us so much. If we want to please God, we must love Him back, and our fellow men too."

A man shouted out, "We want to love Jesus and follow His fashion too."

One day they came and said, "We are not learning fast enough. Please will you teach us every day? We will come in here at midday." So a daily mid-day meeting was added to the already full programme of meetings. There were seventeen meetings a week, and some were attending most of them regularly. There were days when Ivor spoke five times. Then on Saturdays he trekked out with each of the local preachers in turn to encourage them.

Another day in reply to the question, "Why did Jesus, the all-powerful One, allow Himself to be killed?" someone said, "Jesus wanted His blood to run to the ground so that He could wash away our badness. Then we would not have to go to Hell, but could go to Heaven."

There were other reactions too, for we were not just teaching stories about a good man, but were also fighting a battle with the unseen forces of evil. Satan had held undisputed reign over the Yuna for centuries and was not going to give them up – not without a raging battle anyway.

Never before had I been so conscious of the presence of evil powers as that first night we slept in the Pori Valley. After a near fight among the carriers I felt scared, not only frightened of the untamed men all around us, but conscious of other forces too that did not want us to come.

Ivor too spent many hours in like battle when he was here alone, particularly at the time his tent was burnt down. "The demons did it," the men around him declared, and he was left in no doubts about their presence.

Many times during the meetings in the early days some man would have a type of fit. He would begin to tremble violently. Then, grabbing an axe, bush-knife or whatever happened to be handy, he would charge about suddenly among the seated group. The message disrupted; the crowd would scatter until finally some of the men would pin him down. Often after a while he would move off and sit down by himself. They were disrupting, frightening experiences.

Evil spirits were not to be taken lightly or dealt with by the inexperienced. Once a man tried to cast a demon out of a woman. While he was praying he put his hand on her shoulder and was thrown to the ground. When he regained consciousness, he found that she had committed suicide. In Acts, when some power-seeking, self-glorifying exorcists tried to act in the name of Jesus they were themselves overpowered. "Jesus I know, and Paul I know about, but who are you?" the evil spirit asked. (Acts 19:13–16). Only as the Lord gave discernment and clear instruction could action be taken against those spirits.

One missionary among the Yuna witnessed one of the fits just mentioned. The victim was a young man whom he knew. Standing near him he prayed, then commanded the evil spirit in the name of Jesus to leave him alone. Immediately relieved, the lad looked up and said, "Thank you, sir." Ivor had similar experiences.

These 'fits' only occurred in the early days of the work. Later, when there was a preponderance of folk in the meetings who had turned away from worshipping the evil spirits, they ceased. But we noticed them each time we moved into a new area.

One day Ivor was preaching in a centre several hours' walk away. Afterwards a young woman who had been showing an interest for some time came and asked for an injection.

"Why do you ask for an injection?" he asked her.

"Because Satan is inside me," she replied.

"An injection cannot cast out Satan," he replied. "But God is stronger than Satan. I will pray to Him. I will not give you an injection."

After praying he felt no freedom to cast out the demon. He questioned her to see if there was anything wrong physically, but she affirmed that there was not. A few days later she was carried in to the station unconscious. Again, we could find no medical reason for it. Her husband and others said, "She is not sick. This is Satan. We have seen it happen many times. We used to offer sacrifices to him. Sometimes there was instant recovery. Others died after a few days."

After more prayer we too were convinced. One of the leaders, a Christian, was standing by. Ivor asked him to pray and then cast out the demon, and he did so. The next day the woman was back working in her garden. Others who looked on believed. This battle with the powers of evil was reality. We saw it too often to retain any doubts. Satan tried to deceive Christians into believing that he did not exist.

Yet how triumphant we felt when we saw the changed lives of these people, men and women, being liberated to declare the glory of God through our Lord Jesus Christ.

4

FEAR OF THE DEVIL

For we are not fighting against people made of flesh and blood, but against people without bodies—the evil rulers of the unseen world, those mighty Satanic beings and great evil princes of darkness who rule this world; and against huge numbers of wicked spirits in the spirit world.

Ephesians 6:12 (Phillips)

In Sickness

"For two days now our son has complained of a headache. Today his skin is hot. His breath is puffing. He is no longer able to eat or walk." A hoarse cough followed by a whining cry came from behind the woman's back. She sat down cross-legged among the sweet potato mounds, and lifting the string bag from off her head, swung it around in front of her, gently lowering it on to her thighs.

The crying and coughing increased. She opened the bag and pulled out a six-year-old boy. He looked plump and healthy, but was burning with fever. His breathing was so fast that a diagnosis of pneumonia could have been made on the spot had anyone been there who understood.

"The evil spirits are grieved again," the distraught father muttered. "Will we never be free of their bondage?" He looked on without seeing as his wife sought to comfort the child in her arms. The boy was shivering violently now as the damp and cold settled on his hot body. "Pigs, evil spirits, pigs," the father mumbled on. "I have killed many pigs in order to be freed of the spirits' tormentings. Once I had so many pigs that I was considered wealthy. In fact, I had enough to buy another young wife as well as feed us all. Now they are gone, gone. All killed to appease the evil spirits.

"First, my wife nearly died, after the last baby was born dead. She recovered once I found out which spirit was aggrieved and made a sacrifice to it. Then this son of hers was sick a few moons back. Three pigs were sufficient that time. Again, the best sow was sick. She died, but not until I had wasted several pigs on her. I was not able to find out in time which of the spirits was aggrieved." His wife's cries penetrated his gloom. "Our son will die. See, his sickness is a big one. The spirits are very angry again. Hurry, sacrifice!"

"The blood of all my pigs has already run. Why are the spirits always angry with us? Perhaps your brother will spare a pig to save his nephew's life. First I will go and call the spirit man to find out which spirit is responsible," he replied.

"Go with hurry," the mother's voice reached a hysterical crescendo. "Go, before my child dies as all his brothers and sisters have done." Her wailing followed him across the expanse of gardens as he went towards the sacred bush. Others heard her too.

Soon a group of women gathered around. There was much talking and wailing, all of it pregnant with fear and despair.

The father explained the situation to the old spirit man and then waited while he went slowly into the sacred bush. Time seemed endless. But wait he did, for he dared not disturb the old man's communion with the spirits. The wailing of the women reached his ears from across the gardens. Was the child already dead? Would the old man be able to ascertain at once which spirit was aggrieved? Why, oh why, had they picked on him again?

Finally, the old man emerged and named a certain spirit. Relatives were persuaded to offer a pig and more futile sacrificing went on. Two days later the child died. A mother of eight was now again childless. The death-wail echoed all over the valley as groups of women converged on the burial ground. They milled around, crying, wailing, beating the coffin with sticks and calling to the spirits to leave them alone. The mother kept coming back for days to sit near the putrid body and wail and pray to the spirits.

Bringing a patient in on a stretcher

Traditional tobacco smoking

Evil spirits and fear, despair and fear, sickness and death, and fear, fear, fear.

This was the pattern of life or, more often, death for the Yuna before they received medical help and learned to pray to a God who answered prayer.

Medical work played a vital, essential role in the work here. Often it was said to us, "If only we had medical help, we would stop sacrificing to the spirits when we are sick."

We tried as soon as we arrived to get them to bring in their sick ones, but at first they were afraid of reprisals by the spirits. Gradually, though, they started to come in with sores and wounds, and we began to build up their confidence. But still in cases of illness they continued to kill pigs. Then late one wet afternoon a woman came in with a semi-conscious two-year-old. He had had pneumonia for several days. A number of pigs had been killed, but he was no better. We prayed with the mother, then went to treat the baby. When she found it was to be an injection she was again too afraid. Finally, we said, "This is it. We must give it and break through this barrier of fear." So holding the mother as well as the child the needle went home and the magical penicillin started its work. The following morning she came back beaming. The child was drinking again. The temperature was normal. This time she willingly submitted to the injection being given and our medical work was under way.

The story spread all over the valley and they started coming. Only a few at first, but soon it snowballed into quite a good-sized clinic each morning. By far the greatest number of cases had pneumonia. Babies got hot and perspired freely in their bed of leaves in the string bag. Then when they woke, their mother just sat down where she was, often in cold wind and rain, to suckle the child. They would carry a sick child in their arms in the wet and cold rather than in the warm and dry bag because they were fretful – so many of them died as children. From talking with the older women it seemed that the infant mortality rate must have been about 70%. Over and over it was the same story repeated, "I have had eight children, only two are living."

One of my first patients was a little boy with the end of his finger chopped off. "How ever did you do that?" I had asked.

He did not answer. Finally someone said, "His father did it." Then, noting my expression, he proceeded to explain, "It is our custom to do this to children who, after a couple of warnings, continue to steal."

"Oh," we said.

We had noted with appreciation that the Yuna were not thieves – an unusual virtue among tribal people. With most, the only wrong is to get caught.

After a few months, I often came to recognise what the complaint was, simply by looking at the clay markings on their bodies. If the pain was in the chest, it would be striped with grey clay like a zebra. If, on the other hand, it was an abdominal pain the markings would be vertical and lower down, as well as great welts from using stinging nettle as a counter-irritant. For a headache they would hit their foreheads with a sharp stone and then rub red clay into the bleeding cuts.

For influenza or malaria there would be stripes all over the arms and legs as well as the body. This, of course, was all connected with their fear of the spirits – an attempt to ward them off.

Every time a person or baby had a severe illness their name would be changed, in the hope that the spirit would not recognise them again.

The people placed great importance on prayer for the sick. In the clinic we prayed with the sickest ones individually every morning. In the more distant areas, they finally came to the point where they were willing to cease sacrificing pigs to the spirits, even though they were too far out to get medicines. They told us many stories where we believed, with them, that the Lord healed their loved ones without the use of medicines.

Just a few months after we settled here, a very sick lad was carried in to us – a boy of about fifteen who had come over to Koroba to carry for us when we walked in together. Now he was the size of an eight-year-old. His hair was gone, his skin scaling off. One thigh was twice the size of the other one. A swelling had started two months before just above the knee and had gradually extended up his thigh.

A conversation with Dr. Sturt confirmed my fears of a fast-growing cancer and we had to tell the people that we could do nothing. It was a big blow to the young fellow, one of our workers, who had persuaded them to bring him to us. He had been trying for months to get them to bring their sick ones in. This was the first one they brought. I could have given him a course of penicillin, but was so very short of it that I felt I should hold it for babies with pneumonia.

So they carried him home again. The young workman so lost face that it was weeks before we saw him again.

Then two months later the patient himself walked in to see us. He was well again. His hair was growing, his skin shining, he had put on a stone in weight and his thigh, though still slightly swollen, was giving him no trouble. His only complaint was that it was heavy.

Many people had been praying for the lad and they believed that the Lord miraculously healed him. What looked like being a real stumbling-block to the people of his area became the turning-point in their decision to begin a search for God.

The Women's Story

I was anxious to get in touch with the women as soon as I arrived at Pori, but how to do so was a problem. Many of the men were already receiving daily teaching when Ivor had a meeting down on the airstrip where they were working. The women were getting nothing.

My permit to be there stipulated that I was not to move anywhere without Ivor. The women were too frightened to come to the mission station, which was fast becoming the meeting-ground for many strange men. The women believed that if one of the men so much as looked at a woman he could perform sorcery that would cause her, or her child, or one of her pigs to become ill and probably die. So they remained hidden in their gardens, growing sweet potatoes and tending babies and pigs.

Although the area was de-restricted just the day before I came over, thus rendering the conditions of the permit no longer binding, it was still necessary to be very discreet. One day I took a cup of tea down to the airstrip to Ivor and looking across I saw a group of women starting a new garden quite nearby. Here was my chance. I moved over and called to them. Rather frightened, but too curious to run, they stood while I approached, making friendly greetings in the few Yuna phrases I knew.

Then one of them answered me in Huli and I realised that they were bi-lingual, and so, talking to them in Huli, I was able to have my first women's meeting. Sitting in the middle of the garden with just half-a-dozen of a congregation, I started.

"God is the Great Good Spirit," I told them.

"God," they repeated after me.

"God is strong. God is good.

God made everything – sun, moon, ground, food, pigs, people.

The evil spirits are strong, but God is stronger.

The evil spirits are bad. God is good.

God has one Son. His name is Jesus."

Then we went over and over the same ground a dozen times until they could say the name of Jesus and God (Yetu and Ngode) and answer questions correctly on the above facts. It was a thrilling beginning and soon I had contacts with several such groups.

Eventually they took courage to come in to sell food to us. They always came in groups and I was able to play over for them a tape recording of the previous Sunday's sermon. Of course, they were not always able to stay and listen, and they were never pressured into staying. That could have earned them a beating for not finishing the day's gardening.

Some months later, we were able to persuade the men to allow us to hold actual meetings for the women, and then, being able to move about the valley with a trusted escort and interpreter, I commenced four meetings a week, one in each direction from the station.

On Sunday morning the call would echo around the hills, "*Tuguli kua, tuguli kua.* Come to school, come in order to learn. Come and hear God's talk." In the first months a handful of men turned up and no women. Their menfolk had told them that they would beat them if they dared to come. Religious things were strictly for men. Women were to stay in their place of absolute subjection, working for the dominating males.

If they came, they or their children might get sick and die. This was more than a threat – evil spirits have power to cause sickness in those who worship them.

We prayed. Folk at home were praying. Ivor had many long quiet chats with the men pointing out the need for them to become united Christian families. Finally, one sunny Sunday morning, Hibuya brought three of his wives and their daughters. Timidly, they sat out of sight over the brow of the hill. How we prayed that no tragedy would strike.

Our prayers prevailed. Each Sunday following, a few more and more were there, hiding just over the brow of the hill, out of sight of the men but within hearing distance. They always crept in late and left early, but mostly they listened.

As I sat with them each week, I learned their names and watched their reactions. Two faces began to stand out. They seemed to be drinking in every word, and always hushed others who might be inclined to chatter.

One was Berabu, a girl of about nineteen, wife, and mother of a lively one-year-old boy. Her husband, Arali, worked for us, chopping wood or carrying water. Early one morning, I happened to have been looking out the window just as a terrific shout rent the air. I saw Arali drop two buckets of water he was carrying and rush off over the hillside.

Someone had shouted out to him that Berabu was out in the bush trying to hang herself. She was demon-possessed. Binding her up with vines, it took several strong men to drag her home and tie her to a tree. There she stayed bending low over a fork in the trunk with her hands tied low so that she could not get her teeth into the vines that held them.

Days and interminable nights succeeded each other until she was sane again. Clad only in a grass skirt she survived, unharmed by a climate where it nearly always rained every twenty-four hours and where we used three blankets inside a house. This happened quite often and each time she was there three to five nights.

She continued to attend meetings, drinking in every word. With her keen mind she was always quick to answer questions regarding last week's sermon. I wrote to prayer-partners asking for prayer for her. She seemed such an outstanding personality, with real leadership potential. Gradually a change came in her demeanour and attitude. She had been well known for her quick temper and vicious fighting. Now these traits were coming under control, but the bouts of demon-possession were more frequent and intense. Satan was fighting to a last stand for her soul.

One day she and Arali came together and took a clear stand for the Lord. She showed a radiant personality and transformed way of daily living. How would she continue? Who would be victor in her heart now? Many who had known her so well in the past were watching. If Berabu was really such a transformed person, then this Christian way of life was reality.

Early one morning there was more shouting. Looking out the window we could see that Arali's new house was on fire. And, yes, the word came in that someone had seen Berabu putting a torch to the grass roof. Arali was furious. He dragged her down the hillside, kicking and abusing her. But she was not insane, they said. Arali assured us that he had done nothing to anger her.

She absented herself for several days and then one morning when Ivor came in for morning tea he said, "Berabu is outside."

I went out to find her hiding shamefacedly around the corner. I led her gently inside and we sat down on the kitchen floor together, to try to get to the bottom of it.

"Has Arali been unkind to you?" I asked.

"No," she replied.

"Were you angry with him about something?"

"No."

"Then why did you burn his house down?"

Her answer was that something had just made her do it. That morning when she got up she had not been thinking unkind thoughts towards her husband. However, when she went outside and looked at his new house, something inside her gripped her and made her go and set it alight. She was very ashamed and had put it right with Arali and the Lord.

So we prayed together, claiming complete deliverance in Jesus' Name and through the power of His shed blood. The Lord answered prayer.

Several years passed and Berabu was still going on for the Lord. That dynamic personality was now His and she was a real leader among the women, the humble servant of all.

Had God changed? Of course He had not and neither had Satan. The battle was still a spiritual one, and God's touch still had its ancient power. He was Victor.

The other face I particularly noticed among the women who hid over the brow of the hill those first Sunday mornings was that of Gebogone, a younger girl, third wife of one of the most influential of the headmen. She was about sixteen, and so very different from Berabu. She was sweet and quiet, yet there was a certain strength of character about her that impressed me. Her heart just seemed to open up more and more to the Lord's love each week. She absorbed all she could get to hear.

One week we were visited by a Christian Huli family from Tari. It was the first time the Yuna people had seen a united indigenous family living together and showing harmony in their lives as they followed Jesus. They had a very healthy-looking two-year-old boy. The wife spent many hours just sitting chatting with a group of women around her. After a few days there was a conversation that went something like this:

The Christian wife: "When I had my baby I performed none of the pregnancy rites of evil spirit worship!"

"What?" the local women replied. "You never had the old women pray over you, asking the spirits to protect you and give you a live healthy baby?"

"You never put clay markings on your abdomen?" another asked.

"No," she replied smiling, "I only prayed to God."

"But he's a big healthy boy," someone pointed out wonderingly. Some of the older women showed real disapproval.

"We have never done anything to appease the spirits when he was ill or even to ensure that he grows properly," the Christian wife continued.

There was more excited, disapproving jabbering and the matter had been discussed by all in the ensuing days. Quietly and thoughtfully, Gebogone sat listening. Later she went to the couple for a long personal chat. She told them that she believed all that she had been taught about the Christian way of life. She wanted most sincerely to follow God's way and obey His 'talk'.

"I am pregnant," she went on. "Can I really forsake all the old spirit ways and trust God alone for my health and my baby?"

They encouraged her and prayed with her. Then she came and told me that she was determined to go through with it.

Almost daily, she came for reassurance and to pray together. There were many hurtful incidents when the old hags of the tribe tried to intimidate her. They did their utmost to get her to allow them to pray over her, to ensure the spirits' approval. She was endangering others, they said, for the spirits would certainly have their revenge on someone.

I wrote home again to those I knew would pray her through and she held on. One day one of the old spirit women said to her, "Your baby is dead."

Startled, Gebogone looked at her for a minute. "What do you mean?" she asked. "It is not dead."

"Oh yes it is – or it soon will be," was the reply. "I saw you washing yourself. Washing! With warm water! Of course your baby will die."

Gebogone made the short trip down the hill to our house again. "Would you please listen to the baby's heart?" she asked.

Always ready to reassure her I complied. Then she told me what had been said. We prayed and she left again, her radiant, confident smile speaking assurance to all who were watching her so closely.

At last a beautiful daughter arrived. What a triumph for the Gospel! All over the valley people were saying, "Truly God is greater than Satan."

One morning ten days later I woke to the sound of wailing. "Who has died?" I asked.

"Gebogone's baby," came the staggering reply. Yes, God had taken the wee one home to Himself. How hard it was to understand. Certainly it was all according to His perfect plan for the parents and for the advancing of the Gospel among the Yuna, but just how was I supposed to speak to the parents? After prayer with Hope Dobbie, I went up the hill to see them.

There was Gebogone sitting in the garden with the tiny body on her crossed legs. How my heart ached for her. Crying to the Lord to take over my tongue, I sat down beside her. Silently, I wept too, and the tears flowed down my cheeks. Then, stammering, I tried to speak to her. It was not long before women began to gather. Groups, ranging from five to twenty, came in from various directions, all wailing. What an indescribably miserable, eerie, high-pitched noise they made. As they finally approached, Gebogone silenced them.

"Please don't wail," she said. "I have finished with all that old way." They looked at her in wonder and amazement, some obviously quite unable to comprehend. Then she went on, "My baby is in Jesus' arms. She is happy there, she will never be sick, never feel the pain of being beaten. And one day when I die, I am going to Heaven too and I will see her again then."

The women were awe-struck, silent. I too was silent with my own thoughts. Just how would I have reacted, with all my background of teaching and knowledge of a loving Saviour? It was a tremendous rebuke to me. And it was a mighty challenge to all who witnessed it. There were many women present that morning who first decided to forsake the old spirit ways and then went on with the Lord.

Berabu and Gebogone went on to have a tremendous influence. Gebogone persuaded others to come for ante-natal help and to leave off the spirit worship that the old women tried to force them to perform. So we started a maternal welfare programme. The decision was a spiritual one for them: it involved a completely changed attitude in everything to do with their personal lives, their babies and young children. It meant looking Satan in the face and saying a clear-cut "No!". And it meant holding on in faith through all the fiery darts that he hurled at them day after day in their own thoughts, and through the old women, who sensed that they were losing prestige and power.

Berabu's changed life spoke volumes. Together, they persuaded many to leave off doing the old things and come to the meetings to learn a new way. The group grew until there were a hundred attending each Sunday morning and coming in just as often as they could during the week to hear Sunday's message played again on the tape recorder.

There was no word in the Yuna language for 'wash'. Water was a very dangerous commodity, to be drunk in small quantities and never to be deliberately applied to the body. When I gently suggested washing their babies they looked at me aghast.

"But they will get sick and die!" someone said in a tone that said, 'Unbelievable'. Occasionally I repeated the suggestion. I knew they had no means of heating water and no soap or towel.

Late one afternoon, I was struggling with a smoky fire when I heard a voice at the door. I saw the face of a woman who had recently come to live nearby. She was holding a chubby five-month-old baby boy, naked and very dirty. "Here," she said nervously holding him out to me. "Wash him." A few others were standing curiously behind her. It was a sunny afternoon, so I took a basin of warm water outside and an old towel. The child came to me happily and chuckled with delight when I lowered him into the warm water. Drawn faces relaxed into smiles as I splashed the water over him and he continued to show his pleasure. Only one old lady continued to glare, muttering awfully to herself, or more likely to the spirits. I rubbed him dry and handed him back, still smiling his delight to his mother.

No ill befell him and a few days later three others were brought in to be bathed. Soon I was spending one morning a week bathing and dosing with cod-liver-oil, weighing the babies and any other older ones who were not doing too well. On the whole, babies and mothers were healthy here in the Highlands; there was very little need for bottle-feeding.

Gradually they learned to do the bathing themselves. Gebogone and Berabu became my helpers, handling the big laundry tubs of warm water, and teaching each new mother to get behind ears and into chubby creases. I would talk mothercraft all the while, and then hold a Gospel meeting after the baths were over. Soon there were hundreds coming and they had to be divided into groups to come in turns.

The general medical work had a big influence on the women's story too. They came with their sick babies and saw them get well – so many had died in the past. When Sister Betty Gillam joined us at Pori in September 1967, the Maternal-Infant Welfare Programme got into full swing. Smaller clinics were held in the various centres throughout the valley with attendances ranging from thirty to eighty. Up to eight hundred babies were checked monthly and given the usual immunisation. Ante-natal clinics were held at the same time, followed by a women's meeting.

We had not had a lot of midwifery work to do. For a while when the women were first becoming Christians, they felt a real need for something to replace the full programme and magic and spirit appeasement that they had been bound to. Hope Dobbie had the patients come in to the station. She trained three Christian women, Berabu, Gebogone and Gubwa to come and sit with the mother and pray with her, encourage her, and come for help if it was needed. Afterwards, they left mother and babe clean and comfortable. This was a great encouragement to many to make the break with the old pregnancy, child-bearing and child-raising rituals. Now they no longer came in to the station, but had their babies at home, helped by the more mature Christian women in their home area.

What a contrast to the old ways! Previously, when the baby was due, the father might build a tiny hut away from any other houses. The mother-to-be would lay in a supply of firewood and perhaps a little water, though once in labour she would stop eating and drinking. Then she would be left to sit in there alone, no-one wanting to go within earshot of her. It was a frightening experience for a 15-year-old having their first baby, especially with her mind tormented by all the stories and fears she had been taught.

No one was allowed to see the new baby. He was carefully hidden away in a string bag on a bed of leaves. Father's eye could cause sickness during the first three months. Only one or two trusted female relatives could share the mother's joy.

A great change had now come. People sat with her and prayed with her, she was waited on, and her husband was there waiting for the news. Almost immediately, he would go in and see his wife and baby and they would pray together, thanking God for His gift and seeking His blessing on them as a family.

Yes, the Yuna women came to trust God – many of them without any reserve – and had passed from terrible fear to glorious freedom.

A Girl's Life

Wani stirred and realised the birds were singing. She rose, stepped round her mother's snoring form and began removing the slats from the doorway. The outside air was cold but preferable to the smoky, fetid atmosphere inside the low windowless shack. The ridge of the house was only one and a half to two metres above the ground, the thatching went almost down to the ground and the walls were only about a metre high. The smoke of a fire smouldered in the centre of the dirt floor, providing their only warmth in a climate where the temperature occasionally dropped to less than 8 degrees. They had a name for frost, but it was a rare sight. Hail was more frequent.

Wani inhaled great gulps of fresh air and looked around. The grass was heavy with dew. In the east a great mass of scarlet cloud heralded a fine day. Birds twittered and called overhead. Smoke oozed through the thatch of neighbouring houses. Looking up, she noticed that the bananas were ready to cut, though a bat had been at them during the night. Down below the house, the mist was a swirling mass, filling the steep valley above the river. She shivered, then heard her father's voice speaking kindly, "Feed the pigs, Wani, and let them out of their house."

"Yes Father," she said, moving to obey. As she returned to the house her mother handed her a sweet potato, hot out of the ashes where it had been all night. They smiled at each other. Family life had not always been like this, she remembered. Not before they became Christians. Then there had been anger and beatings, pain and rebellion and tears, frustration and fear, fear, fear.

After the missionary had come to live next door, her father had worked for him on the airstrip. As her father watched his life and listened to his teaching, he had begun to change. At night, when he had eaten his sweet potatoes and greens, he tried to pass on to them what he had seen and heard during the day. Often he was confused, but gradually Wani came to understand a little here and there.

On Sundays she went and heard for herself. Not many women were allowed to go. Religion was the men's business and the women always had work to do. Some of the men were saying that the others who let their women go to the meetings were soft, and that they would rue the day when they had started to treat them thus as equals.

When the missionary first came, he persuaded the headmen to let some of the little boys go away to school. Hibulu, Wani's older brother, was one of them. As he left for Koroba, Wani and her mother wailed, wondering if they would ever see him again. The other side of the mountain was another world away. Later, when the younger brother died, and a new baby was born dead, Hibulu came for a holiday and they kept him at home to live with them again.

"Hurry up and eat, Wani." Father's voice brought her back to the present. "Today we are going to start a new garden up beyond the big road." As the early sunshine warmed the fog and penetrated through to the valley, they started off up the track together.

Truly Christ had made life a changed experience for the Yuna women. The underdog who did all the hard work, bore and often buried the babies. A woman was beaten and thought no more of than a pig. A woman's soul was equal only to that of an animal. A man would be as grieved over the loss of his good sows as he would be over the death of one of his wives.

A daughter was wanted often not so much for her own sake as for the bride-price that she would bring. The pigs brought to her father would buy him another young attractive wife. More wives could grow more food and feed more pigs and bear more daughters – and then even yet another young wife could be had. Thus was wealth and prestige gained by the older men. A younger man often had to start with a widow or divorcee for his first wife, the price being lower.

Family life was non-existent. The husband had his own house and each wife hers. She slept in it with her daughters, babies and pigs, suckling the pigs' young as well her own if necessary. If she had a small baby the one breast was kept for it and the other for the piglets. Babies were suckled for several years and then the boys, at about six years, went to live with their father.

By the time Wani was seven she was expected to work all day with her mother. Before that even, she had duties of watching that the pigs did not stray, and of keeping an eye on her younger brother. Now she was considered big enough for a full day's work.

After the men had cleared off the scrub and topped the trees, women and girls dug the ground with their sharpened sticks, then heaped it into mounds with dry grass and ashes underneath. Later they planted sweet potato runners in them and kept down the worst of the weeds. When it rained in the afternoons they just carried on with their pandanus leaf capes thrown over their heads and backs. Late in the afternoon, they gathered a full bag of sweet potatoes and a stack of firewood, staggering as they returned home with the load. The dried gourd shells had to be taken to the spring and filled with water.

By now Wani was an expert at blowing up the fire from the apparently dead embers. After peeling, the sweet potatoes were carefully pushed under the hot ashes, and a pumpkin baked whole in this way, or unpeeled corn cobs, were added to make a delicious meal.

She had few playmates — not that there weren't any other little girls about. It was just that they were all as busy as she was.

She saw them and called to them across the garden as they worked and sometimes they walked home together. They always went together for water, for a girl must never be alone.

One day when she was about nine, a young man approached her mother and said that he would like to 'mark' Wani. Did Wani like him? "Yes," she assented shyly. He gave her mother a present for her, some red beads and a piece of mother-of-pearl shell on string, a love charm, ear-pendant.

The next day was Sunday. Father had not been told about the betrothal, but during the service up on the missionaries' front lawn he suddenly noticed the adornment. "Who gave you those?" he bellowed, right through the sermon.

"Patarali gave me them for her yesterday," the frightened mother replied.

"Why wasn't I consulted?" he roared. Jumping up, he pushed through the group of seated women and snatched them from her face, then turned and threw them at Patarali. The women all started to talk at once, and Wani hid her bleeding earlobes in her mother's lap and the men hooted their amusement in derision of the women. Ivor eventually restored order.

Such incidents no longer occurred. Wani's father was still a strong man, respected and listened to. Understanding and gentle, he was well able to handle a blundering young man out of a heart full of love. Her mother too was gracious and loving.

In fact, Wani's parents were the first couple to confess Christ. They had real shepherd hearts and an unofficial ministry in the young churches. Wani became a sweet Christian teenager. Later she was also baptised.

A Man's Life

It was preferable to be born into the male side of the Yuna society. Certainly, a man's life was still one of fear and bondage to the spirits, but it was much more his own than was a woman's.

At first, he lived with his mother. As a toddler he still suckled at her breast and was never for a moment out of her care. Never smacked or disciplined in any way, he always got what he wanted; he could scream in a tantrum for hours if necessary. It was great! All the women would gather around him and he was the centre of attention. It never failed to work.

When he was about six, he spent much more time with his father, and after a while went to live with the men. Now he listened to their talk — filthy things, fighting things, fearful things. He quickly grasped the attitude of male superiority and domination of the women. He was cheeky and very rude to his mother. That was fun too, because everyone laughed at him. When he realised it was another way of getting attention, he did it regularly.

As he got a little older, he ganged up with the other boys of his own age and lived a completely carefree life — shooting birds with his little bow and arrows; securing a humming beetle on to the end of a string without killing it, and buzzing it all day long; raiding bird nests, and playing for hours with the half-dead creatures. He made a non-bouncy ball out of the pith from inside a palm tree, or fastened the top of a tin can on to the end of a stick and pushed it along. There was always food for him when he wanted it. It was just a matter of blowing up the ashes and pushing in some sweet potatoes to bake there. One thing he could not get away with was stealing. That, repeated too often, could mean the loss of a joint of his finger.

It suited him well (at this stage anyway), that his parents believed that if they punished their child he would not look after them when they were old. Father sometimes did lose his temper and thrash him mercilessly. He never associated with girls. They feared his arrogant bullying and dirty tongue and kept well away.

So the years went by until one day he and his elders realised that he was starting to grow up. Now he must settle down a bit, do some gardening, learn to make weapons and fight, take part in spirit-worship, and begin getting pigs together for a bride some day.

He went off with the men to prepare a new garden area. They topped the biggest trees and felled the rest, leaving high stumps. On these they heaped the long grass and scrub as they cut it. When the whole area was half dry they burned it off. Sometimes it had to be lit several times before it was well cindered. But they were not satisfied with the fast fire of a thoroughly dried area.

Now the women took over and worked the mounds and planted the sweet potato runners. Women were useful after all, he thought. He decided that he would have to accept them a little, and work in with them at times.

It was great fun going with the men to fight. At first, he was made to stay at the back of the group. Usually one group were on the one side of a valley and the enemy high up on the other side. Then one group would charge, firing arrows as they ran, whooping and shouting and calling insults to the fleeing ones. Then they reversed and everyone ran in the opposite direction. It was exciting. Quite a few got hit with arrows and sometimes one or two died. That made him afraid. Nevertheless, he was always thrilled to hear the men working themselves up for another flare.

He had got a few pigs together now, and various female relatives were caring for them in separate places. This meant that if anthrax broke out in one area he would not lose his whole herd. It happened once to the ones his mother was caring for. As each one sickened it was killed. They were eating meat for days. When his cousin, a few years older than he, was ready to be betrothed, he gave several pigs to help. The cousin would do the same for him some day.

Yes, some day he would marry. He began noticing the girls. But should it be a girl? Perhaps a widow would be a better worker, and better behaved too. After all, he only wanted a woman for the sake of the work she would do and the children she would bear. He had no thoughts of romance or companionship with her.

Another year or two went by and then he heard through the grapevine that a certain girl was interested in him. He prepared a love-charm and offered the present to her. She accepted. Her father agreed to negotiate. Now he was here, there and everywhere, persuading relatives and fellow clansmen to help him get together enough pigs. The girl's father was pressing high. He wanted eighteen pigs, six of them had to be sows, several of them grown but young females; some piglets would be counted in. The day before the appointed time for the payment there was excitement all over the district and a noisy herding of pigs. Now that he had them all together, he was anxious to get rid of them before something happened to any of them.

When the pigs were officially accepted by the girl's father, the transaction being witnessed by many members of both the clans concerned, the girl became his property. Literally - property. Now she was spoken of as his wife, though as yet she was only a fiancée.

Now she would work gardens where he said, and she was expected to work hard, probably living with his mother, though this was not necessarily so. There followed several months of ceremonies and spirit-appeasement in preparation for marriage. The older men saw to it that he was fully equipped to ward off any evil that might come to him once married. For women did have some power over men. They had potent ways of attack, and powerful sorcery.

With all the ceremonies completed and the gardens bearing, the old men would inform him that it was nearly time to consummate the marriage.

Now he decked himself in a full range of bridegroom's apparel. On his head was a large, beautifully decorated wig, his wrists were weighed down with fertility charms, and special feathers and leaves were stuck through the armlet on his upper arms. Large strings of shells hung down his chest and a snake-skin stretched across his forehead. A white pig tusk stood out against his blackened face, and he carried a large powerful bow and a handful of arrows and deported himself proudly as he moved around all over the valley, giving everyone the opportunity to look at him.

At last came the final gruelling test. His friends rallied around him to keep him awake. Day and night they took turns to keep him moving, keep him awake. How long could he last? After five days it was best not to speak to him, and after seven it was necessary to keep out of his sight. Then at last he was ready to take his bride.

The young couple had their moments, but he was well able to assert himself. Once, when she didn't get through the required amount of gardening, he beat her, and broke her forearm, the accepted form of punishment.

He didn't take her to the hospital for an x-ray and plaster; he simply ordered her back to the task on hand. Another time she allowed a wild pig to rip a young piglet she was looking after for him. A heated argument ensued, and he finally sat her into the bed of hot ashes. That taught her. Yes, he was a good husband and doing all the right things, and she was a good wife when she finally bore him a daughter.

He was accepted now as a mature man, and spent many pleasant hours just talking around the fire in the men's meeting house. Gradually he was acknowledged as a leader of the warriors when they went into battle.

One day a strange white man came to live nearby. He worked for him and heard his talk. He learned some fantastic things and drank in every word. What a transformation took place when he and his wife grasped the message and, confessing their sin to God, were accepted by him! No fighting any more. He came to love his enemies and went out of his way to teach about the Saviour who had transformed his own life.

And a wonderful new relationship had built up between him and his wife. They ate and prayed together and talked things over. They were baptised together and attended literacy classes to learn to read. He was happy for his wife to attend the women's preacher-training class and to go out to help teach other women. She now co-operated to the full without any bullying, and they lived, worked and worshipped together.

5

FREEDOM IN CHRIST

In the past you were spiritually dead because of your
disobedience and sins… You obeyed the ruler of the
spiritual powers… But God's mercy is so abundant…
he brought us to life with Christ… he raised us
up to rule with him in the heavenly world.

Ephesians 2:1–6 (GNB)

First Fruits

January 1964 – July 1969

Tere was a thin grey-haired old man. He came gasping and wheezing up the hill, stopping every few yards. One of his friends had died, and he was determined to get to the funeral. Besides, he just had to see the white missionary again. Some of the men, and his young son too, were telling him of the fantastic things that the missionary was teaching. He wanted to hear for himself.

Old Hiwi was dead. They had shared many battles together, as well as many evil spiritual rituals. Now where was his friend? They told him that the missionary said that the spirit goes right away from the earth after a person has died. It went to one of two places, once of which was good, the other bad. Where had Hiwi gone? At the back of his mind he was aware that his turn could not be too far away. That made him fearful.

Hiwi's funeral was the first time Ivor noticed Tere. He looked old and frail as he sat there listening intently to a message – "After death, where?" Afterwards, Ivor made a point of chatting to him, referring to the message he had just given. Then, putting his arm around his shoulder, he said, "What of you, Tere? You are an old sick man. It may be your time to die soon."

Tere looked up thoughtfully and concerned. "Truly I am old and sick, but I live right down in the gorge by the river. My bones are not strong. (It was his lungs). I can't get up to hear God's talk very often," he said.

"Then one day when you are feeling strong enough, come up and we will sit down together and talk," Ivor invited him.

Only about a week later he came, driven by a searching heart and even more urgently by an aching tooth. Puffing, with great beads of perspiration trickling down his face, he arrived at the back door. I had not seen him before, but guessed who he was and called Ivor. As soon as the old man saw Ivor he said, "My tooth is eating me. Please will you pull it out?"

He eased himself down on to a large flat stone and I handed him a drink of water and a couple of aspirin. He looked up gratefully and my heart went out to him. "Lord, reveal Yourself to him and bring him to a place of repentance," I prayed silently.

Before tackling the tooth, Ivor squatted beside him and with Pita, the fourteen-year-old interpreter, talked for a long time. Tere drank in every word and asked questions. It seemed that the Lord was just opening up his mind and heart. In His love, He was giving him this opportunity to turn to Him.

"They nailed Jesus on to a tree," Ivor said. "He died for you, Tere."

"Did the blood run when He was dying?" questioned the old man. All his life he was used to the offering of animals to the evil spirits, so he knew the significance of blood sacrifice.

"Yes, the blood of God's Son ran for you and me. He died, but because He was God He rose again three days later."

As the interpreter passed that on to him, his face just shone.

"Truly God is strong," he said. "Since you told me about Him and about Heaven and Hell, I have known that I must prepare to die. I am very old. I am thinking a lot about Jesus. I want God's way."

Obviously, the Lord was working in his sin-darkened old heart. Ivor explained the need for a personal acceptance of Christ. The old man then said, "I want to pray to Jesus and ask Him to clean my heart."

And so he did. It was the first spontaneous prayer we had heard in Yuna. The tooth came out without difficulty, and he tottered off. As he left with his face just beaming he said, "I'm going to my house. I'll tell my friends about Jesus. I'll send my son to hear your talk and he can come back and teach me more. I'm going to finish with praying to the spirits and killing pigs to them, too. I'm going to pray to Jesus and go to His land when I die."

We were amazed. He had had so little teaching. It was just the simple working of the Holy Spirit in his heart.

Next Sunday afternoon we went down to his house and received a spiritual uplift from the visit. He was thrilled that we had come. After chatting a while he said, "I used to be afraid of the spirits, but now Jesus is in my heart and He is looking after me. The fear has gone. I pray every day and great happiness is with me." Tere had moved from fear to freedom.

He lived on for nearly three more years. Once, when he was low physically, unable to crawl out of his house and confused in his mind, he asked his son to do what had been considered a son's duty. "Please cut me with your axe," he said. Some time before, he had had the timber prepared for his burial box. It was stacked near the house where he saw it daily. His son came and told us what his father was asking him to do, so we went down to chat with him. He pleaded with us, "Please pray that I might die. I do so want to go and be with Jesus. I don't want to stay on here like this, trying to die and going on living."

However, it was not his time yet. He made quite a good recovery. Sometimes he managed to climb the hill and come to services, though more often he just stayed in his house bearing a radiant testimony to all who came to see him.

Once, when Ivor was visiting him, he said, "If they come and tell you I'm dead, you'll know that it is only my body. My spirit will be with Jesus in Heaven. Goodbye, brother."

How wonderful the Lord was to extend His mercy even to those whose lives had been almost fully lived in evil ways.

Tere especially influenced a number of the other old men; those in his own age group who too had lived lives full of evil. No doubt that is why the Lord did not take him quickly to Himself. He went to the Lord later, however, and his old bones became strong again. What a wonderful Saviour!

God's love is like the sunshine,
   It covers land and sea.
It fills my heart with gladness,
   When I know that God loves me!

Patarali was a bright young lad of about seventeen, who came to work for us soon after we arrived in Pori. He caused many a laugh, brimming with the joy of living. It was he whom we nick-named 'the clown'. Nevertheless, he was an earnest lad, too. When he learned, "Honour your father and mother," he asked for a week off to go and chop firewood for his aged mother.

It was not long before he was standing in front of others, passing on the Bible stories that he learned each week. Then one afternoon, he came and, perched on the edge of an old tin trunk in Ivor's office, gave his heart to the Lord. He was the first of the local preachers to come. He asked Jesus to cleanse his heart and believed that He had done so.

Two weeks later, he went for a trip a long way from home and stood up to preach to folk whom he should have hated as enemies, according to the other members of his clan. They threatened him with sorcery, and he was terrified. He told us that he trembled all over as he looked into their faces. But crying to Jesus for strength, he found freedom and joy in testifying. In this way another clan heard for the first time of a God who loved them and the message came to them through the lips of an illiterate eighteen-year-old boy who had found the Saviour only two weeks earlier.

One day he came and said that he was going to the coast to work. The Government would recruit labourers on behalf of plantation owners around the coast. The labourers were flown out, checked medically, and then they signed on for two years. So Patarali left. But he did not leave our hearts and prayers. He was an illiterate newborn babe in Christ. How would he stand?

Eventually he came back home. He was thrilled to see everyone and to find the tremendous change in the life of the valley, with so high a percentage now Christian. But he found it desperately hard to settle; he just couldn't stand the dirty, stuffy, smoky houses after the clean, if hot, houses at the coast.

After a few days Ivor had a long chat with him. He told Ivor many evil things that he had learned while away. He had continued to pray and to think about the stories he had learned for a while, but his spiritual life had eventually faded out through malnutrition. Mainly, it seemed, he had kept himself pure, though gambling had gained a hold on him. At one time he said that he had had so much money in his rucksack that he was afraid he would be murdered for it. He had not brought cards home with him – he was not interested any more . Rather, now he was keen to learn more. What a change he saw in his relatives and friends! Their whole way of life was transformed, and watching them created a real hunger in his heart.

We persuaded him to join the literacy teacher-training class, though he never committed himself to teaching. He was restless. We held on to him week after week, and he was top of the class. Frequently he came saying that he was going back to the coast, and finally he did go. Where to? Even more pertinently I should have asked, "What to?" If he was in a place where he could get spiritual help, he should certainly have gone on. Even if not, God was able. He was the Lord's, and He promised to keep His own.

I have a Saviour who's mighty to keep,
   Mighty to keep, mighty to keep.
I have a Saviour who's mighty to keep,
   Fifty-two weeks of the year.

Pita: The beginnings of this man's story have already been related. As a young lad he went to Koroba with the policeman and then asked Ivor for work. For some months he worked for us at Koroba, blackening tea-towels and boiling the wash in a rusty drum. Then Ivor, realising that he was God's choice for an interpreter for the advance into Yuna-land, concentrated on teaching him Bible stories and Tok Pisin.

As soon as the advance into Yuna-land commenced, little Pita became the key man. Every conversation that Ivor had with anyone, every sermon preached, every instruction given to a workman was dependent on Pita's faithfulness. It meant that he was on call all day, every day. He slept in a hut just a few metres away from the back door.

His knowledge of the trade language, Tok Pisin, was still very limited, though he was learning fast. Ivor got used to him and could tell quite accurately when he was getting the point across and when he was not. This of course was vital to relationships with the people at a time when tremendous tact and care were necessary.

Then Tiaga, the Government-trained medical orderly, started to relieve him on Sundays and special occasions. This was a great help, as he was older, with a very good voice for controlling a crowd.

Pita got very tired at times and was very difficult to handle when this made him irritable and contrary, but he was always responsive. Though he had his ups and downs, there was always deep down a real desire for the right things. He went away to think and pray and respond when corrected lovingly about something.

It was about this time that he asked us to give him a new name as the old one 'Tongwaiyu' had some spirit connotation. We didn't have to think long to choose Pita (Peter), for him. From that time, he went through the experience of denying the Lord—and then over a period of time responding again to his love.

Pita had had more teaching than any other Yuna in the valley. His enthusiastic temperament took him to peaks of spiritual achievement, only to crash down into a deep valley beyond. At one time he took a definite stand against dances and love-houses. Two of the other workers stood out with him and after a while the whole group decided to do the same.

The dances were the sort that went on all night and lasted for up to three months. They were full of spirit-worship and appeasement, and upset the whole social and economic structure of the community, as folk were up all night, every night. Gardening was neglected, tempers were frayed, and fights occurred, to say nothing of the immorality.

The love-houses, too, were night affairs where all the single girls went to "get to know" the men. Hour after hour they sat there singing suggestive and dirty chants. The heathen mind was utterly degraded and filthy.

Pita took a clear-cut stand against it all. He was on the mountain top. But two months later I wrote in a letter home:

"For some weeks now Pita's attitude has been deteriorating, mainly due to continual dancing at night. Tiredness, a bad conscience and, above all, rejection of the Holy Spirit's wooing in his heart, and rebellion against the Saviour that he knows, are the reasons.

As an adolescent, naturally-speaking, he has been rushed into far too important a place. Lately he has been an arrogant, dilatory, self-important boy. Yesterday mid-morning, his blatant laziness and arrogant defiance caused Ivor to shame him publicly. At lunch-time he came in to return his blankets, plates, etc. which we had given him to use. He was saying dramatically, 'I'm leaving. I'm going for good.' Ivor barred the door-way and spoke very sternly to him about his whole attitude and life. After a few minutes the defiance left his face and, bursting into tears, he rushed outside.

After work had finished Ivor and I were down in the garden, and a very changed boy came to talk. He talked for a long time, fully realising his wrong. Then he acknowledged that it was all due to his attending the dances that he had been arrogantly declaring were quite all right for a Christian to attend. Once again, the Holy Spirit has dealt with this boy and he has responded. After prayer he went away and came to work this morning humbly trying to please."

This incident seemed to be a real attack of the Devil just as the first break was about to come. The next night the first of the local preachers, Patarali, came to the Lord. And from there on, the ones and twos came in increasing numbers. Pita was a tremendous help in the personal work that had become a daily matter; thoughtful, careful as to how he put things, and willing to be called at any time. Often, after Ivor had been talking back and forth Pita would say, "I want to say something else." Then he would talk with the person about something he knew existed in their life that Ivor was not aware of, or he would point out to them something that could be a temptation to them in their particular circumstances. Then if necessary, he would help them in their first prayer, prompting and encouraging.

Over and over again through the years we praised the Lord for Pita, though we had many painful moments dealing with him and shed more than one tear over his conduct.

Later it was discovered that he was a leper. He was sent over to the Leprosy Hospital at the Methodist Overseas Mission station at Tari. There he received excellent care and Bible teaching for some months before he was returned to us, non-infectious, for out-patient care. He was absolutely regular in coming for his Dapsone pills twice a week, fully realising the importance of this. As the leprosy was diagnosed early, he had never been really ill and had no disfigurement, but had of course not been able to work full-time for us.

He married a fine young Christian girl and was happy with her – then once again the shine went off his Christian testimony. Proud and rebellious, often depressed and miserable, he attended meetings if he felt like it, and was surly and hard towards us.

The months went by and then he announced that he was going to buy a second wife. He had quietly gone ahead with arrangements with the parents of a girl who lived a day's walk away. Now he called on his relatives to help him take the pigs through that he was to pay over in a few days' time.

By this time the young churches had come to the point where they were not countenancing polygamy. Some polygamists had been baptised, but one of the conditions of baptism, decided by leaders of the churches, was a firm statement by the candidate that he would not take further wives. They were, though, expected to accept responsibility for those that they already had, and especially their children. The standard of one man, one wife, was definitely accepted as the only one for the future.

The leaders were disgusted with Pita. His Christian relatives refused to drive the pigs for him. However, he found enough helpers to get them together, ready for the marriage payment.

As the leaders inquired further, they found that the girl's relatives were among a group of people who had recently started to forsake the worship of evil spirits and to seek after God. So they went out and talked with them and explained what the Bible taught about marriage, and they said immediately that they would not go ahead with the negotiations.

To say that Pita was angry would have been a gross understatement. For several weeks he was never seen without his bows and arrows strung up and ready for action. Ivor tried to talk the thing through with him, pleading with him to let the Lord have His way, but the only result was deeper rebellion and hate.

He blamed us for interfering and breaking up his negotiations. In actual fact, it was all done by the elders themselves of their own initiative, though this was, of course, as a result of our teaching over the years. One morning he came in when I was alone. It was Sunday morning when Ivor and all the workmen were out preaching and everyone it seemed, except him, was attending the services. But Gerene, a local elder, had seen him coming in and quietly slipped out of the meeting and followed. As he stood at the door talking to me about some trivial matter, there was Gerene standing quietly but solidly nearby. Finally Pita went off to shoot birds.

This state of heart went on and on for many months. Then he and his wife lost their first baby which was a stillborn and she nearly died too. It was a big shock to him and the first indication we had of a changing heart was when I saw him sitting there in the maternity hut holding his wife's hand and praying with her.

Gradually since then – over about eighteen months – a change came. There was a new light on his face, and he regularly attended meetings where he humbly took an inactive part. He learned to read and was always ready to help, when called on to do so, in interpreting or helping to teach others to read.

The Lord later gave them a lovely baby, and it was a thrill to see his tenderness with his wife and his devotion to the child. It was very precious to them both. Still a young man, there was much he could accomplish for God.

Make me a captive, Lord,
And then I shall be free;
Force me to render up my sword,
And I shall conqueror be.
I sink in life's alarms
When by myself I stand;
Imprison me within Thine arms,
And strong shall be my hand.

My will is not my own
Till Thou hast made it Thine;
If it would reach a monarch's throne
It must its crown resign;
It only stands unbent,
Amid the clashing strife,
When on Thy bosom it has leant
And found in Thee its life.

George Matheson

Reaping a Full Harvest

Towards the end of 1963, eighteen months after settling here at Pori, we became aware of big changes. The entire culture of the Yuna and Huli people around us was changing. Inter-clan fighting had completely ceased, murders were rare, fewer women were coming in to have their heads sewn up after fighting with gardening sticks, hundreds of the people had stopped making offerings to the spirits and many had ceased to pray to them or consider them at all.

Several hectares of gardens had been planted near the mission station. Previously, the people had lived out in the mountains, scared to stay down in the more open valley after dark. Now there were houses and gardens everywhere. People who had been in hiding a full day's walk away had lost their fears and had come back to live on better ground which they had previously forsaken.

In the spiritual work, barriers of fear and superstition were crumbling all around us. Twenty preaching-points were established throughout the valley and the faithful local preachers went out every Saturday and Sunday to teach the story they had learned during the week. Two thousand people were regularly hearing the Word.

Early in September, we had a visit from a group of dedicated Christians from the UFM area at Tari, and it was during that visit that the big break-through began. Their ministry came at a vital time. Many people wanted to come to Christ, but had reservations as to whether this was really something that would work for them or whether it was something just for the white man. Then they saw Christ in the transformed lives of people just like themselves. The visitors were Huli, who had a very similar culture to the Yuna people.

The first prayer-meetings were held. Thirty-five men and nine women gathered daily in separate groups, everyone taking part. The first married couple (Wani's parents) came to confess their sin and get right with God. This was the first woman to confess Christ.

Over the week-end, eighteen official meetings were held, reaching 2,500 people with a total attendance of over 4,000. More than 1,000 people gathered on the station for the final meetings. After their visit, our weekly programme of meetings doubled: daily Gospel meetings, enquirers' classes and prayer-meetings were being included.

Several weeks went by with a small group of people coming to the Lord each week. Married couples, family groups, consisting of a man and two or three wives and some older children, would come together and pray individually in front of each other getting right with God.

One of the things that fascinated us most was seeing their transformed faces during those weeks of reaping. Each Sunday morning as the crowd gathered, Ivor and I would watch them and speak to them. We saw faces change, transformed with a new light of hope in place of fear as they found themselves rid of the burden of guilt and the fearful power of the evil spirits.

Just on Christmas Bob and Hope Dobbie came to join us. Bob came ahead and worked with Ivor on a little cottage. As soon as the place was completed, Hope and the children came in too. They settled in and took over the preaching and teaching programme, enabling us to get away for a holiday. We were kindly taken in by Alex and Evelyn Sinclair of Goroka. Warmly welcomed into their generous hearts, it was a wonderful Christmas for us, a real break from the constant pressure of the work and the people.

Refreshed, we returned to the most wonderful week of our lives, a week in which a hundred people, Yuna and Huli, came to acknowledge Christ as their Saviour. For some, it was the occasion of their first prayer; for others it was the public confession of a transaction that had already taken place. For that week we did nothing else but talk to people. Meetings were held as scheduled with no time for preparation and no work was done as the interpreters and the missionaries spent all their time counselling those enquirers.

One morning I stood and listened as one of the leaders tried to put people off from coming. Stress had been put on the teaching that there must be individual, personal acceptance of Christ. He said over and over again to a group of twenty people sitting on the grass beside him, "Do not come to talk to the missionary unless you personally mean business with God. Do not come just because your wife or husband or sister or aunt have said that you should. Are you personally meaning this?" Not one of them left. All were dealt with individually.

Family groups, couples, single people, elderly men and women, they came and they came. At first we were afraid. What was this? Was it really of the Holy Spirit? How could we doubt? Hourly, miracle after miracle was taking place before our eyes. It was a tremendous experience of being guided of the Holy Spirit in conversation. What was said to one was not the best means of approach for another. We knew relatively little of the individual lives of the people we were dealing with, so the Holy Spirit gave us the words to say to each one in turn.

After that week they still continued to come. Sometimes they came to us, but more and more they went to those who had been Christians for a while, asking for counselling and help in learning to pray. One day, during the women's prayer meeting, I heard several speak openly who had never taken part before. Each was a prayer of confession, asking for forgiveness and cleansing. Some months later, they told me that that was the time when they were born again. I had nothing to do with it. As they stammered fearfully trying to find words, one or another of the Christian women would speak up to prompt and help. For a long time, our prayer meetings were like that, with continual interruptions as those who had been Christians for a few weeks helped more and more of their friends to learn to pray.

Ivor sharpening a saw blade

Sawing logs by hand

The First Fetish Burning

The aged evangelist stepped into the circle of a thousand pair of eyes and stamped triumphantly on the heap of fetishes that had been placed on the ground. It was January, 1964, just a couple of weeks after the week when a hundred people came to the Lord.

Earlier in the morning a noisy procession had passed our house. Being carried shoulder-high, there were squealing, struggling pigs, wood, stones, bunches of leaves, bamboo knives, wooden clubs and bags and bags of vegetables. A small group broke formation and came to speak with us. "We've brought our fetishes," they whispered awesomely. "We do want to burn them, but will you pray for us first?" Their hearts were burning with a mixture of the old Satanic fears and the newly-found joy of liberty in Christ.

After reassurance through prayer, they all moved down to the site that had been cleared for the first Christian feast. Members of enemy clans were to meet as brothers and sisters and eat together out of the one oven. Formerly, when the ovens were opened, the food was taken home to eat. They would not eat in front of others for fear of sorcery connected with food.

Nineteen pigs were slaughtered, all well bled and completely without ritual. With bristles singed over the fire, they were then cut up, following a definite routine. Most of the butchers were young men, with the older men standing behind, correcting them now and then.

As preparations continued a light rain set in. We asked the Lord that the day would not be spoiled by rain – a day scheduled to be a witness to His power and glory. Soon the clouds lifted, and a cool overcast day ensued. Fires were lit to heat long rows of broken limestone, and a long shallow pit was prepared. Men and women were still coming with more and more bags of vegetables. Sweet potatoes, corn cobs to be steamed with the leaves still on, green bananas, pumpkins to be cooked whole, local spinach and tender young bamboo shoots – all were placed near-by, ready.

As I stood up at the house and watched, the tracks were lined with people streaming in single file from every direction and corner of the valley. Soon there were well over a thousand talking and laughing, greeting each other, waiting expectantly.

The stones hot, and the meat butchered, all was placed into the pit, protected by leaves and then covered in with dirt, and left to steam.

Order was called and everyone sat down in a huge semi-circle on the playing field at the top end of the airstrip. Piru, a guest evangelist from Tari, spoke forcefully. A ceremony followed which finally marked the great change that had come in the culture of these Yuna tribes-people. One after another, the men came to the front and placed their fetishes on the ground—unusually-shaped stones, shells, pieces of certain plants, all of which had been for them very special and terrifying. They had thought that each one of them was the dwelling place of evil spirits, and had believed and feared that Satan himself was enthroned in some of them. He had been reputed to perform mightily and frighteningly through ritual associated with these things. The women had never seen them before. Now these senior members of the tribe were saying dramatically that they were finished with all that.

Large, terrified eyes gaped from the crowd as the aged evangelist stepped out, trampling the fetishes under-foot and shouting, "God is greater than Satan. We no longer fear him and his evil spirits." The eyes of Christians watching held a look of real triumph. After prayer, all the fetishes were collected up and placed on the fire.

Then there were races and games and good fun until at last it was time to open the pits of steaming, delicious food. A prayer of praise and thanks was offered, then a portion of the meal was placed on leaves in front of each group of people. Ivor moved around with a great bowl of salt sprinkling a little on all of it.

A relaxed, cheerful atmosphere prevailed as these former enemies ate together, and as the sun's rays began to slant, laughing, chattering groups fanned out all over the valley with joy in their hearts. Many were acknowledging the God who had given them freedom in place of the old fear.

Establishing Churches

"Home to New Zealand, and into hospital!" the doctor said.

"But surely...we can't leave the work at this stage. Who is there who could possibly relieve us?"

But the doctor was right, and we soon realised that I would have to go, immediately. Once again the Lord worked, in a series of miracles. We had little more than ten NZ pounds in the bank and we needed 450 for fares alone. He sent it, and He sent someone to help the Dobbies to carry on with what was now a heavy load of teaching and building-up of all the new babes in Christ.

However, this is not our personal story: perhaps I'll tell that another time.

I flew south, and Ivor followed three weeks later. In the meantime, Kerry McCullough had come, and Rae was to follow before long.

We were home for two years. In that time, Bob, with his real teaching ability, built a knowledge of the great truths of the Scriptures – line upon line of simple, consecutive teaching until the Christians were rooted and established in the faith. He taught them on subjects like the "True Nature of Sin", God hated sin, we were all sinners. God told us what His standard was and none of us could meet His standard, but God loved the sinners, and He sent Christ Jesus to redeem us. Christ was the only remedy for sin; repentance followed by conversion was possible only through faith in Him and His death and resurrection. All these facts were taught, slowly and with much repetition.

The next stage was "Going on with God", or "Growing up in Christ". The fact, power and presence of the Holy Spirit; prayer, and the Scriptures; a mind fixed on God; the fruits of the Spirit, which were evidence to others of the changed heart within – love, joy, peace, patience, kindness, goodness, faithfulness, gentleness, self-control; these things, too, were taught.

It took many months. Appropriate memory-verses were translated and taught until they had a coverage of every point etched permanently on their minds. It was thrilling to watch individual progress. Over the months, dozens of folk demonstrated that they were indeed "new creations in Christ" and "growing up in Him".

Only now, on the evidence of radically changed lives, did Bob and Ron Whitehead go ahead and introduce the subject of Baptism. Several months were spent in explaining its significance. Baptism was an outward confession that an inward transaction had taken place, a public declaration that the individual had once and for all left all the things of the old life, and now had only one desire – to go on with God.

Finally, our health restored, we came back to Pori. Hallelujah! I can't even begin to describe our joy as we looked into the transformed faces of hundreds of people. Over and over again we had to ask, "Who is that?" And then, when told the name, "Really, he or she is so changed that I didn't recognise the face."

As Ivor visited them and enquired everywhere about their changed way of life, it just seemed that nearly everyone was living a changed life; the vast percentage of them were truly born again and going on with the Lord. We wept for joy.

The teaching on baptism had been thoroughly given. Bob and Ron had appointed representatives, or interim elders, in each group of believers and these men were receiving preacher training. They had been taught to look for the evidence that a person was ready to be baptised. Now they were asked what they felt was the standard requirement for baptism, in this culture, in line with what they had been taught from the Scriptures. They prayed and talked and asked for more help from the Scriptures. "What does God say in His Book?" was the persistent question as they sought to reach decisions.

They would have been happy for the missionaries just to say, "You must and you must not," in a demanding, legalistic way. However, that was not the right way, so we waited and encouraged them to learn to take responsibility and make decisions according to the directing of the Holy Spirit in their hearts, as they applied the Scriptures to their Huli-Yuna society.

It was their decision to require a quitting of smoking. Hundreds of tobacco plants were destroyed. Polygamy, too – each man was asked how he felt about taking more than one wife. Then, in a society where there were few secrets, wrong relationships at home could not be hidden, and were not passed over. Control of children was more difficult. Girls, yes, but to know where the boys were and what they were doing was not easy. Nor did they seem to be able to insist on them attending services at the mission of the parents' choice. However, over the following years improvements were made.

Eventually they listed the names of those who they felt were ready for baptism in their particular groups. Now the missionaries and representatives together spent several weeks questioning those listed. Sometimes it was one at a time and sometimes in family groups that each one was questioned as to their faith and understanding of the doctrine of baptism.

At last, the date was set for the first services. Wednesday, 17th September 1966, dawned cool and overcast. As we prepared to leave the house we could see and hear hundreds of people moving to the central point. They were all delighted when we joined them. Hope Dobbie carried the baby in a sling in front of her, and her toddler was perched high on their wash-girl's shoulders. Our Lynette was on a young man's back in her car-seat strapped to an ex-army carrying frame. Richard was carried by our house boy. Still another young lad carried a flour drum with lunch, raincoats, a change of clothing, etc.

Three quarters of an hour brought us to everyone's destination – a natural amphitheatre packed with two to three thousand people, seated and looking down on a pool of muddy water. We scrambled down to be among them.

After a short meeting, there was a tremendous hush as the first man stepped into the brown water and across to where Ivor was standing—the first of eighty Christians who obeyed the Lord in baptism during that service. In one week six hundred were baptised in six services in different places. They were grouped in numbers ranging from 60 to 325. Each spoke a clear testimony and voiced a determination to go on with the Lord.

In each place Ivor and Bob baptised some of the more mature Christians first. Then these stayed in the water and helped, sharing in the joy and privilege of baptising their own relatives and friends. Those baptised were mostly married couples. Quite a number of grey heads went under the water that week, some single men, and a few single girls.

A former fighting chief gently helped an old lady down into the water; a grossly-deformed man, formerly believed to have been conceived by an evil spirit, had given evidence of having been born of the Holy Spirit; women formerly controlled by demons, feared for their fighting, but who were now known for humbly serving others. Purua, the spirit-man who confessed to having communed directly with Satan, stood in the chilling water with a towel and wiped people's eyes as they came up out of the pool.

On the next Sunday morning, all gathered in several groups for their first Communion Service. Its orderly, reverent procedure was only possible after much teaching. No one had ever witnessed such a service before; no one could read and nothing could be more different from their former way of doing things. It was a steep, thatched-roofed chapel, the walls 1.3 metres high and open all the way round above that. The floor covering, if there was any, was woven matting made from flattened-out bamboo; the people crowded in, sitting cross-legged on the floor – women on one side with their babies and toddlers and men on the other side. In the centre was the table, made from hand-adzed planks, uneven and far from level, but it held the little cane baskets of sweet potatoes, and the dried gourd shells of raspberry juice. A reverent hush pervaded the three hundred and twenty-five people who gathered there. Every heart was bowed before the Saviour who had wrought such a change in their lives. It was a tremendous joy to witness such a spectacle, and impossible to explain what it meant to us – how much more to the Saviour Himself!

The daily Bible class continued. Now it was more of a preacher-training class, as representatives came in from each church group to learn the story and the application to be taught at the meetings of the coming week. Sometimes the same people came in each week. In other places they took turns, a different preacher being appointed for each week.

Imagine how hard it was to prepare a sermon when you had no concordance or commentary, no Bible, not even a story book, and you couldn't even read. Teaching continued to be in story form, with the message attached to it point by point. Then, as the preacher recalled and retold the story, so he remembered the application, having heard it at least four times over the past few days and he was able to give something worthwhile to his hearers.

Consecutive teaching was given on various subjects. One month was spent taking four lessons from the letter to the Ephesians; another few weeks covered the life of Abraham. Then, over Easter, five weeks were taken to cover the stories from the Last Supper to the Ascension. From there it was a series on the life of David. Thus the building-up went on slowly and thoroughly. It was a great thrill to watch their delight as they heard some of these tremendous stories for the first time. Of course, all the basic ones were taught in the early years, but some of the stories in a series such as the life of David, for example, were new. What drama and what lessons there were in them. A greater thrill was to see them appreciate the message of the story and respond to the challenge in their hearts and daily lives.

They asked some thoughtful questions. After the Easter series one man said to Bob, "What happened to the Jews' scattering and suffering in more modern times?"

The "representatives", or interim elders, continued to serve and came in weekly for detailed instruction, based on Scripture, for the conduct of the local churches. There were many problems to sort out. How they would have appreciated the easy way out — a legalistic approach. However, we said "No". We will teach you what the Scripture teaches. You yourselves must apply it to your culture, make decisions and take actions on your own initiative." At first, it was necessary to give a fairly positive lead in most situations, but more and more the missionaries receded as the local men took responsibility on to their own shoulders.

The First Elders

After weeks of teaching about the qualifications for eldership, such men were officially appointed in each church group. The representatives were given the teaching each week and went back to pass it on. How it must have searched their own hearts.

Personal qualifications—blameless, temperate, sober, of good behaviour, patient.

Moral qualifications—not self-indulgent, not violent, not materialistic in outlook, not argumentative, not quick-tempered.

Social qualifications—a happy home, right relations with wife and children, hospitable, well-thought-of by non-Christians.

Spiritual qualifications—a mind fixed on God, a lover of good things and good men, mature, a godly man, good knowledge of the Scriptures, a good teacher, a man ready to be the willing servant of all. (From 1 Timothy 3 and Titus 1.)

At first, such ideas were utterly strange. The qualities of leadership that they had acknowledged before were strength of will-power and personality, to be able to bully and boss and fight. The one who could talk loudest and longest was the one finally listened to. Love? Peace? Humility? Yes. They saw it. This was the way of life. This was the way of freedom from fear.

The exercise of discipline was a problem. Some were all for firm action that was good in doctrine but lacking in grace, so that the wrong-doer was turned away rather than won back to the Lord. Others were hesitant to take definite action where it was needed.

The biggest difficulty of all was the question of polygamy. Most of the mature men were already married to more than one wife when they yielded control of their lives to the Lord. The standard of one man, one wife, was definitely set, but there was never any question in their interpreting of Scripture that they should put away the wives they had already taken. They and their children were a responsibility to be taken seriously. Some of the men who were acting as interim elders were polygamists. They had been told long before that they could not be appointed as official elders. Now it was a joy to see the humble, joyful ways these men accepted their position. Most of them did a great work in a quiet way, counselling and helping many who looked up to them with real respect because of the lives they lived.

In some churches it was obvious who would be the chosen ones; in others, because of polygamy, they were forced to appoint one or two rather young ones. Though warned about this, they felt it was the right thing to do.

Finally, when we felt that all understood the teaching given, they were left to continue in prayer until one by one each group reached a unanimous decision before the Lord as to who they felt were the ones the Holy Spirit was appointing for them. The decision was theirs, not the missionaries', though in most cases we were in whole-hearted agreement with the decisions they reached. A very high standard had been set, as there had been for those asking for baptism. We were gladdened to see it. It was much easier to set the highest possible standard at the beginning than to try to raise it later.

Decentralisation

From the immediate area around us, three hundred and twenty-five people gathered at the mission station each Sunday morning. We felt it was too many for one group and we did not want to have a mission station church. There were four local churches meeting at the Huli end of the valley and four among the Yuna. Now Ivor broached the subject of decentralisation. These local churches contained several clan groups. Why not find one local church for each clan? At first, they were a little disturbed. "Why?" one asked. "Do you want to get rid of us?"

"We would not have enough men able to preach," another said.

"Each group of you has men capable of preaching," Ivor pointed out. "They only have to come regularly for instruction and then make a start. They will soon learn to stand up and pass on what they have heard. Besides, you should be witnessing right in your home area to your relatives and friends. You should build a chapel for yourselves and stand on your own feet. You are mature men. You can't go on leaning on others!"

After a few weeks of prayer and discussion they began, one group at a time, to see that this was the reasonable and right thing to do. Group by group, they built chapels on their own home ground and started meeting there. Now many more men were carrying responsibility and developing as preachers and teachers.

One morning we all went to Eroyango local church. The chapel was just a few minutes' walk from our house – in fact, we could see it from the kitchen window. About nine o'clock, they shouted down to us that everyone was there. They kindly did it like that because they had no clocks and meeting time varied as much as two hours, being later on a wet morning.

A large group of women and girls flocked around the kiddies trying to say their names. 'Lynette.ee' was not too hard for them, but 'Richard', or 'Witch.it.ee' as they said it, sounded a bit odd to our ears.

We greeted each of them, having a word here and there. One lady looked so sick that I checked that she had been down for medicine; there was also an elderly lady who was going down-hill fast. She just sat with her head on her drawn-up knees, taking in little of what was going on. Yet she roused herself to take of the emblems during the communion service and mutter her thanks to her Saviour. I knew she would be with Him soon.

One little girl had grown so much that I commented on it, much to her mother's delight. Then to another young mother, "How many teeth has this one now?" How they loved us to notice their little ones.

But it was time to go inside for the Communion Service. We wriggled in among the women seated on the dirt floor. They loved our kiddies and it was impossible to keep them from being a distraction, however quiet and good they were. The men were all on the other side of the building.

Someone prayed.

Another said, "Let us sing 'Into my heart' as a prayer, with our eyes shut." 'Jesus come, Jesus come, come and abide with me'—they chanted rather than sang, having a range of only four notes.

Another prayed.

Someone recited a selection of memory verses, with the group responding line by line.

Then Ivor read to them Mathew 5:23–24: "So if you are offering your gift at the altar, and there remember that your brother has something against you, leave your gift there before the altar and go; first be reconciled to your brother and then come and offer your gift."

It was not the first time that they had heard that teaching, but the Lord wanted them to hear it again. The day before there had been a long discussion and argument about the routing of a road out to one of the outlying chapels. All were keen to put this through, except two men who refused to allow it to go through their land. Many who had been involved in the dispute now spoke to one another.

"Was I angry with you?" one asked.

"Should I take the emblems?" asked Hibuya. "I was angry with them. Was it anger with sin in it?" After thinking a while, he decided that it was righteous indignation and that he was holding nothing against his Christian brother. Others talked about it and then there was a time of special prayer before proceeding with the service.

Several prayed, and then there was a special prayer of thanks for His precious body broken, and the sweet potatoes were handed around. Another prayer of thanks was offered for His shed blood, and the raspberry juice was handed around. Each bowed in prayer after partaking; some prayed silently but most in a quietly audible voice. What a joy to hear those grey-haired old women voicing their love of, and appreciation to, their Saviour!

Literacy

They need...

    To read...

        To heed...

A drop of ink makes a million think!

Yes, the Yuna people too needed to learn to read. The Ray Browns who had previously settled at Kelabo made a good start with the task of reducing the Yuna language to writing, but then they were withdrawn for more urgent work. Others replaced them, but their work was badly interrupted by ill-health and by other responsibilities. Eventually an alphabet was formed, and primers prepared. An abridgement of Genesis and the Gospel of Mark were translated and printed in trial form. Other missionaries among the Yuna had also worked hard to produce reading helps and Bible stories.

Later, Glenda Giles began giving most of her time to the revision of these and to further translation work.

With the rapid growth of the spiritual work here, the missionaries' time was more than full. Very soon after we returned from New Zealand, several young churches were formed, with not one person among them able to read.

What was the most efficient way to get all these people reading? One method was the 'Each one teaches one' idea. We thought about this, but our observation of the method in actual practice was that without supervision by trained people they simply memorised their books. They noted the illustrations, listened while someone else read the words, and then quoted the page without actually being able to recognise the words.

Having decided that we must train teachers, we discussed the matter with the elders. They were keen to learn to read, keen to start immediately. However, old folk found it hard to learn and they had enough responsibilities. Eventually it was agreed to select two or three mature young men from each established church, practising Christians who would pledge themselves to this task to serve the Lord by teaching others to read.

One morning I faced a class of bewildered but enthusiastic students and wondered how best to handle them. We settled down in no time. Experiment proved that they could not take more than forty minutes of work at a time; they had never concentrated before. In the morning session they would be alert and work well, but when we met again at two o'clock they were tired and lethargic. So the going was slow, and we were determined that it would be sure. Eventually they learned to read. All the time, and more so towards the end of their course, I sought to point out the teaching methods I was using, with the aim of preparing them to teach.

It was a great thrill one morning to see the new teachers leaving after their first briefing class. Each had a blackboard, chalk and rag, and a sheet of foolscap paper with the week's work listed on it. It was all there, set out with just what they were to put up on their blackboard for each day. All they had to do was copy it and then get through to their students. They had flashcards, too.

Thrilled, enthusiastic, and with a real sense of mission, but no real idea of what was ahead of them, they set off to set up their schoolroom in their local chapels, and so the classes started, with one teacher for each of the Yuna churches. Four teachers had been working, under Bob's supervision, at the Huli end of the valley for some months prior to this.

Now my time was fully occupied preparing the worksheets for the teachers each week and the homework sheets for the students. These were a summary of the week's work given out to take home and practise over the three-day weekend. For a start, I visited each class each week, seeing as many as four a morning. Each student was tested and then a coaching class was started here on the station to give extra help to those who needed it. One in six of the students came in, mostly the older ones – grown men, many of them functioning elders; the ones we wanted most to learn, and nearly all were doing well. They were certainly keen and tenacious.

Why?—and How?

Why, and how, had the Yuna people turned so whole-heartedly to the Saviour, and in such large numbers?

There were a number of reasons. Firstly, they were a prepared people and the Lord Himself timed our arrival here. Then they were a spiritual people. They understood something of prayer and spiritual powers. They did not just worship idols and things that they could see, but dealt with unseen forces in the spirit realm.

They were greatly influenced by the transformed lives of Huli Christians. We arranged for several visits by Christians from the UFM area at Tari. The timing of these visits was of the Lord, and, just at the right time, the people here were challenged by what they saw in men and women with the same colour skin and a similar culture to their own. They were convinced that this new way of life was not just some illusory thing for white men only, but a Person, who was a living reality in the lives of men and women like themselves.

The Huli and Yuna people did not do things by halves. They were by nature a whole-hearted people, full of enthusiasm and drive. When they fought, they put everything into their fighting. When they worshipped evil spirits, they did it to the full. When they turned to Christ, they did this whole-heartedly too, seeking a high standard of life and conduct within their ranks.

They were a strong-charactered people. Once a decision was made and the first step taken, they were not the kind to go back on it. The Yuna could not be called submissive, but were perhaps a little more so than some. They had not been a minority group but rather a middle group. Their neighbours, the Huli, were a very big tribe, and used to make their superior strength felt at every opportunity. However, there were also other smaller groups adjacent to the Yuna which they looked down on. Thus they were not crippled by a sense of inferiority, nor by an arrogant spirit of superiority – which had been very marked in some Huli areas.

All these things, however, were secondary to the main reason for the tremendous response of the Yuna to Christ. That reason was prayer. Prayer was the key to success in any spiritual work, and the work here had been bathed in prayer from before its inception. The Lord had blessed us with a wonderful group of prayer-partners. Many of these vital men and women were members of our immediate family circles. How we thanked God for Christian relatives, and united families, who stood behind us. There were many others in New Zealand churches and also others scattered all over the world who prayed for us – really prayed for us.

Some Christians prayed for missionaries just by speaking their names before the Lord, saying, "God bless brother So-and-so and his dear wife today", and that had value, but there was so much more in real intercession for the work. A man who was to chair a meeting for a missionary went to him before introducing him and said, "I have prayed for you regularly. Now tell me, where are you from? Is it Papua New Guinea or India?" He was one of the many who prayed through a list of names each month, but took little interest in the missionary or the work he was doing.

Vital prayer-partners were actively interested in the work. They kept themselves informed. They were inspired of the Holy Spirit in their praying and insistent until they saw the answer.

They revealed their interest when they wrote and said, "How is Hibuya? I pray for him by name daily. Has the fourth wife been converted yet? What of the big daughters? I claim their lives for Him now while they are young, that they might be kept from the evil that their parents have known." That was vital interest.

Then they were informed. They read a prayer letter with a view to gathering material for prayer, not just because it was well written, to be enjoyed and then forgotten. They looked for articles and prayer item lists, and used them. They read a book like this, and prayed as they read it for the people and topics mentioned in it. Many kept a notebook neatly listed so that they would not forget any need that they had read about or heard of.

Of course, no one could have taken the whole world on their heart, but asking the Lord for guidance as to specific missionaries and places to concentrate upon was a powerful way of making a difference in people's lives, including our own during our time in Papua New Guinea. This was possible, for spiritual people were inspired in their praying. The Holy Spirit could control our minds when we were at prayer. Such people knew what it was to sense an urge to pray for something or someone when they may have had no news for some time. Later, they found out that there was a real need then and that their prayer was answered. One friend wrote to say that one day she had stopped her car to pray for me, just right there and then, at the side of the road. She told me the date and time. It was the morning when I was alone in the house and visited by Pita, angry and armed, seeking an opportunity for revenge. I could tell of many more incidents of this kind.

From time to time, I wrote asking prayer for a certain individual or situation. As prayer began to ascend. we often saw Satan descend into the lives of those being prayed for. Usually it meant trials and difficulties as the battle raged – the Lord seeking, and Satan defending his territory. Hence why there was a need for prayer to be insistent. Some battles were won quickly; others continued for months and years. Should we have tired and given in? Woe to the man of prayer who gave in before Satan did! How encouraging it was to know that many did not fail our Lord in this work of intercession.

Reaching Out

There was a similar response at Kelabo to the one we saw here in Pori. Hundreds there began living changed lives and a number of churches were established. The same pattern was developing at Auwi, too, with the first churches already established, but let us go back to the time when there was just Pori and Kelabo.

In March 1964, Ivor wrote a special prayer request to be read at Easter camps and conventions in New Zealand.

> 'For some time now we have been expecting the areas adjacent to Pori and Kelabo to be de-restricted, which will allow missionaries to start working in the area. We are keen that these Yuna-speaking people be reached with the true gospel — others are interested in gaining their ears! As soon as the de-restriction is announced, Ian Armitage will move in from Kelabo, and we will move in from Pori. For Ian it will be a matter of gaining the allegiance of the people and establishing an outpost from which to reach the population over that side.
>
> Down the valley from here there is a somewhat denser population, warranting a full mission station. We will try to locate an airstrip site, get the people's goodwill to let us have the land, and then lodge an application with the Government for the leasing of it. All of our planning is subject to the Lord's direction. We know that His purpose for these people will be realised. Will you join with us in intercession as we press forward? Prayer changes things.
>
> Yours in the bonds of the Gospel,
>
> Ivor Pethybridge.'

After several rumours and delays, the de-restriction was finally announced on 1st August. I was in hospital in New Zealand and Ivor was preparing to follow me as soon as he could.

The Lord knew all along that these would be our circumstances, and He was in control of the situation. The man of His choice was here, ready and waiting to step in and take over what Ivor had been planning and preparing for. His brother Neville had returned early from furlough. The Lord had led him this way, though there had been no indication that we would be leaving until after he arrived. He was here in time to do some Yuna language study and to get to know the young men who were being taught Bible stories, in preparation for going in to the new area to teach.

When de-restriction was finally announced, our missionaries were ready to leave. They found a good airstrip site at Auwi; the landowners were ready to sell, and the Government purchased, and then leased, the land for a mission station and airstrip.

Ian Armitage established an outpost at Arou, which later was linked by road with Kelabo. Literacy and Bible teaching programmes got under way there, with Brian and Helen Telford in residence.

Right from the start, the Christians witnessed well, both by their changed way of living and spoken testimony. Gradually a burden grew to reach other Yuna who were too far out to attend services – folk who, in any case, had not overcome their fears sufficiently to want to attend. The Christians were given help in thinking through the best way of approach and the type of teaching to give, and went out by twos or threes to visit an area known as the Waruni. A lot of time was spent just talking, in gardens, by the side of the track or in the houses at night. In time, one group after another started gathering for meetings when they came.

The Waruni people became interested as they saw the tremendous change in the attitudes and behaviour of these men from Pori. The Pori Christians found the Waruni people to be just as afraid as they had been themselves, unable to break with the spirits for fear of reprisals. The often-repeated question, "What will we do when we get sick?" had to be answered. Gradually, the ones and twos were emboldened to take a stand, and then others followed.

One of the Elders from Pori arrived at a certain place one day and found the people preparing a feast at which to worship the evil spirits. Gelewa knew that they had had some teaching before, and he tactfully got their ears again before they continued with their preparations for the feast. He told them that there was another way of life where there was freedom from fear. "Stop this worshipping of Satan," he pleaded. "Trust God to keep you, and you will no longer be afraid of the evil spirits. Then you too will experience this wonderful new way of life that so many in the Pori valley are enjoying."

They talked on for a long time, and then, to Gelewa's great joy, they said, "We are going to finish with worshipping the evil spirits. We are going to burn our fetishes, here, now, today." So instead of going ahead with the ceremony they had planned, they used the fetish stones to heat the pit to cook the meat which they proceeded to prepare under Gelewa's watchful eye, without any spirit appeasement ritual. (I wonder, who was praying that day?)

Ivor was asked to visit an area ten hours walk away. Some of the Christians there were asking for baptism, their teachers reported. Talking with them, and questioning them, Ivor was thrilled to find how well-taught they were. Mainly this was the work of the elders from the Pori churches. We could confidently leave them to conduct the teaching in these outposts, with nothing more than encouragement visits from a white missionary.

A few months later, a group of twelve were baptised there. There were several such groups, at various stages of understanding within three days' walk from Pori.

It was four o'clock and oh, so cold, with icy rain falling on bare shoulders, and torrents more threatening. The carriers stood with backs hunched, easing the weight of their fifteen-kilogram packs. Their blood-shot eyes showed utter exhaustion.

"*Karu* (enough)", said one.

"*Kewa kone* (tired very)", said another.

"*Tia neya* (no legs)", muttered a third.

No, they were not complaining. But they were utterly down. They had been two thousand two hundred metres up, crossing ridge after ridge of this mountainous heart of Papua New Guinea; ten hours of it had been enough for one day.

It was July 1969, and "They" were a group of Yuna Christians, taking the gospel to their neighbours, the Hewa—a semi-nomadic group, once despised by the Yuna, but now they were lost brothers, to be sought and won for the Saviour. Some of the Yuna had gone there several times in the previous two or three years, and this was the fifth time that they had taken a white missionary with them.

Truly they were well used to mountain-climbing but, oh, those Hewa mountains! Strong muscles were tying themselves into painful rebellious knots. "Enough," the men pleaded, and Ivor was more than ready to agree.

Hibuya wriggled his shoulders out of the rucksack containing the medical kit. He turned to help Rambo out of his carrying pack loaded with a red flour-drum, filled with an assortment of bedding, foodstuffs, Bibles and toilet gear. Now the others were wriggling out of their loads too -salt, matches, razor blades, mirrors and other trade items, as well as their own food. Then they dropped.

There were a few minutes silence before Hibuya lifted his eyes to the approaching thunder-storm and said, "Come on! Up you get. You can't rest here in the cold and rain. Build a shelter, collect a lot of firewood and prepare the food."

Rising stiffly, he began digging post-holes with his axe. With some two and a half metre posts in a row and poles tied to the top of them and sloping to the ground, the house frame was up. A thick covering of leaves made it waterproof, and a big fire made it cosy. Immediately cheered by the blaze, the group gathered behind it and made short work of preparing the sweet potatoes.

After tea, they expressed their love and thanks to the Lord, in a time of devotions, and made intercession for the Hewa people. As the night passed, one or another stirred to push the long logs further into the fire. Ivor was behind them in his sleeping bag, fully clothed, with a heavy jersey and thick socks. Towards morning, someone pushed some more sweet potatoes into the ashes and dozed off again while breakfast cooked.

Bone-weary they all slept until Ivor called to them to put the billy on. One by one they turned over and began talking in thick, dreary voices. Outside it was drizzling and a chilling fog blanketed the entire outlook. So they lingered until nine.

They got going, and improved as the sun broke through, and tired muscles limbered up. It had been the same the day before – descending to heat, climbing to chill heights, they had pressed on. Approaching a river, they could hear its roar and see great boulders the size of a small house moving in the current; it was a relief to find what appeared to be a reasonably new cane swing-bridge. They had lunched on one of the boulders and then crossed without trouble. Climbing up again, they found the other side scorching hot, as they progressed through low scrub. It seemed to go on for hours, without any clean water to drink. Now they dropped down almost vertically to yet another river. It was not as big as yesterday's, but it was unbridged. Holding Rambo's hand in front, Ivor turned to take Hibuya's hand behind. He wasn't there. Where…? Oh, up there. Still on the bank and still praying.

He was not so young now and had always had a horror of swift rivers. With his courage renewed, his life securely in God's hands, he smiled and stepped into the muddy swirls. Waist deep, they stumbled and pulled each other up again as they floundered on the sharp stones. Safely across, it was only a few minutes before they were sweltering up yet another steep mountainside.

So they reached out to the Hewa, and over the next week they spent time with three different groups, making contact with two hundred and fifty interested people. It was strange for the Yuna, especially for one or two single men in the party, to sit in large houses with men, women and children all in together. But their faces were radiant as they told of things they had discovered for themselves, in Christ.

The leader of the first Hewa group said, "We have heard what your teachers have taught us. We want to take on God's ways. Some of us are ready to burn our fetishes. We have arranged to have a big feast tomorrow. We will burn them then, when everyone is here. You will pray for us." Though quite sure of his desire to leave the old evil practices, there was a strong element of fear there as he added the request for prayer.

The next day Ivor looked on and prayed as one after another put his sacred objects into the flames. Many faces portrayed the bondage of fear that was still theirs, but others showed a dawning hope as they listened to a message on the origin of Satan, his fall and his ultimate banishment to the hell which was originally prepared for him and his demons, not for men.

"Christ is Victor over Satan. Christ has power to deliver you individually from Satan's bondage," they were told.

The Christians were tireless in answering questions and talking freely with individuals or small groups as they sat around all day long. They had brought some precious cargo, carefully packed and carried in plastic bags – the Hewa Gospel Recording units. How their faces beamed when they heard a voice that they knew speaking to them in their own mother tongue without the slow progress of a message through interpreters.

They were thrilled. One man was appointed custodian of each set. Small boys were sternly warned not to touch them. Undoubtedly, they would be sitting in their houses each evening from then on, listening and listening until they knew each record by heart.

The leader of the second group said, "We want to learn more. Can't the teachers come more often? My people are not ready to burn their fetishes yet. But they will," he added confidently.

The third group had had more contact than any other. They were Watiaba's people. Watiaba was a Yuna-Hewa bi-lingual, a young man who Ron Whitehead had brought back with him to Pori, a couple of years before. He worked around the station, but lived with some of the Christians, absorbed the Christian message, took a medical dresser's course and learned to read in Yuna. What a difference one could see, arriving here. The people were clean and healthy; there were no dirty sores or continual malaria.

Wagu, the headman, hugged Ivor, and he responded with equal joy. What a joy it was to see such a son in the faith! This group had burnt their fetishes a year prior. By his transformed life Wagu had shown real evidence of being born again. Some day they would be requesting baptism, perhaps forming the first Hewa Church.

Heading off the next day for the long, tough, scramble home, Ivor fell in at the end of the line. As he looked at their backs his heart was aglow. "Loyal servants of the Lord," he thought. "It's not long since we were bringing them the gospel." How terrified they had been to forsake the placating of evil spirits. Now here they were telling others that it is possible to be free of their bondage – liberated by Christ.

But it was very hard trekking. Did they not feel pangs of separation from loved ones? Did they like roughing it in a bush shelter? Aching muscles? Utter exhaustion, to the point of tears? Did any wish they had not come? Surely they were sorry for themselves now?

Ivor listened: out on a more open stretch of country someone started singing. They all joined in:

With my hands I will do God's work,
With my ears I will hear His words,
With my mouth I will teach His ways,
With my eyes I will look to Jesus.
Jesus only; Jesus only.

Marjorie and Ivor with their children, Lynette and Richard, at Wewak

Missionaries of CMML

(now Christian Brethren Churches of PNG) referred to in this book

	Years in PNG	From
Ian & Aileen Armitage	1951-72	NZ
Roy & Nancye Austin	1951-68	Aust
Frank & Beryl Bielby	1959-73	NZ
Colin & Barbara Cliffe	1958-73	NZ
Robert (Bob) & Hope Dobbie	1958-82	NZ
Rex & Gay Eden	1960-72	NZ
Brian & Mary Foster	1961-71	NZ
Elizabeth (Betty) Gillam	1962-72, 81-82	NZ
Glenda Giles	1967 – 1978	NZ
Dick Hedley (s/term builder)	1966?	NZ
Kay & Gwen Liddle	1952-71, 98	NZ
Eric & Marion Madsen	1962-68	NZ
Kerry and Rae McCullough	1959-60, 61, 62-70	NZ
Don & Aileen McGregor	1957-72	NZ
Ces & Mary Parish	1955-77, 82	NZ
Ivor & Marjorie Pethybridge	1960-69	NZ
Neville & Joyce Pethybridge	1959-68, 76-78	NZ
Alex & Evelyn Sinclair *	1958-84	Aust
Dr John & Agnes Sturt	1959-74	NZ
Brian & Helen Telford	1968-86	NZ
Ron Whitehead	1965-98	NZ
Gerald & Betty Wunsch	1951-93	USA

*tentmaker missionaries

Abbreviations

CMML

Christian Missions in Many Lands, the registered name of the missionaries from Open Brethren Assemblies.

UFM

Unevangelised Fields Mission; later became Asia Pacific Christian Mission (APCM) and later merged with Pioneers. The mission assets were passed over to the Evangelical Church of Papua New Guinea (ECPNG).

MAF

Missionary Aviation Fellowship (now called Mission Aviation Fellowship International).

NZBTI

New Zealand Bible Training Institute became the Bible College of New Zealand and more recently Laidlaw College.

www.ingramcontent.com/pod-product-compliance
Lightning Source LLC
Chambersburg PA
CBHW050313010526
44107CB00055B/2226